A BOY'S BROKEN CHILDHOOD

A True Story of Surviving Childhood Abuse

Edward Bruce

This book describes true events that happened in the 1940s and 1950s. Some names have been changed to protect the identities of those involved.

Warning: This book contains graphic descriptions of child abuse.

A Boy's Broken Childhood

First published May 2020

ISBN: 9798646777974

When I was 45 years old I was invited to be a part of a new, young family. Through their love, encouragement and patience I have been able to share my life story with them, which eventually led to me turning my diaries into A Boy's Broken Childhood. I dedicate this book to them.

Contents

Foreword

This book is an account of what I thought to be a perfectly normal upbringing of a boy born in 1940, but who never really became a man until the 1990s. I first met my adopted family in 1985 and as we have shared our lives together, it has become increasingly apparent to us all, that my life had not been very normal at all.

To be adopted by a caring, loving family has changed my life and I dedicate this account to them. I hope that the help and love they have shown to me will be of benefit to others who may relate to some of my circumstances and experiences. I hope that this shows that however bad your childhood is, the power of love can overcome it all and it can turn out well in the end.

As this book is just the beginning of a wider biography, I feel the reader may need an insight to my family's background before I was born in 1940. My family rarely spoke to me about their past so I have a very limited recollection of their earlier lives which I will now try to explain.

My father was born in 1904 in Aldershot and I was told that he wanted to be a minister in the church. However, the family needed money so he was told to apply for an engineering apprenticeship at the Royal Aircraft Establishment (RAE) Farnborough, where his parents worked. He was accepted into an apprenticeship and qualified as a mechanical engineer. He later achieved the status of AMI Mech E, (member of the Institute of Mechanical Engineers). As apprentices were not allowed to stay on working at the RAE after being indentured, he went to work at Gloster Aircraft Company where he met my mother who worked as a tracer there. My father seemed to be well liked by both work colleagues and friends. However the older I became, the more aware I was that the image he presented to them was very different from the way he treated me at home.

My father's parents ran pubs in Aldershot but I only knew his mother as his father died before I was born. She was always known as "Ra-Ra" to me, as apparently that was my first attempt at her name. Later on in my life she became Gran Cally. They had two sons, my father and my uncle Oliver, (Ol) who I didn't see until I was six years old because he was a Prisoner Of War (PoW) during WW2.

My mother was born in 1908 in Cheltenham and was way ahead of her time in so many ways. She became a tracer with the Gloster Aircraft Company and was often given a lift to work by George Dowty who also worked there. Later he became well known when he built his own company and empire manufacturing propellers, hydraulic undercarriages and many other precision components for the aircraft industry. He was later knighted for his services to the country.

My mother used to second her friend Pip Lane who was the British rifle and pistol shooting champion in those days. This took her to many tournaments all over the country. She learned to drive a car at the age of fourteen years and played cricket for Gloucester ladies team. My mother also swam for the county and was also a good pianist, knitter and crocheter and could turn her hand to virtually anything.

My mother's parents were not well off and her father was a stonemason and did a lot of work on Gloucester Cathedral, while her mother was a cleaner. My mother's father also died before I was born and this grandmother was always known as Gran Cook to me. They also had two sons, being my uncles Ron and Den. I didn't see them until they were demobbed after the end of WW2. Ron was a driver for the army in what was then Malaya and Den was a driver for the Air Force at home but was too young to see active service. My mother knew Ron and Den to be of dubious character and eventually found out that the reason Gran Cook never had any money was because they bled her dry to cover their own debts.

I hope this will help the reader to understand my closest relatives.

CHAPTER 1

Early Recollections

I was born on the 14th of July 1940 and christened (I think) Edward William Bruce in a C of E church in Farnborough, Hampshire, where I lived for much of my childhood. I say 'I think' because my parents never spoke about their past, or mine, so this period has always been largely unknown to me. My father was Irish and a big, strong man with a big, strong temper to match. My mother was Welsh and a tall imposing figure who cared very much about her hobbies and pastimes and little else. My mother was 32 years old when I was born, which I believe was considered quite old for a first child in those days.

My parents were a very volatile combination and even from a very early age I was frightened of them. I spent much of my childhood with my grandmothers and they were much closer to me than my parents ever were. The rest of my family consisted of the three uncles I have already mentioned and many cousins on my mother's side. Most of these lived in Cheltenham, Gloucestershire. I only really knew one cousin who was a similar age to me because the family did not tend to keep in touch with each other through choice, only on formal occasions.

My earliest recollection in life was a continuous droning noise while I was underneath the dining room table. I later came to understand that the thick steel plates all around and over the top of an already very strongly built dining room table, created an air raid shelter and that is where I was put to bed for 4 or 5 years. The continuous droning was American bombers, taking off and returning from Blackbush, Odiham and Farnborough airfields. This went on all night because as soon as the last waves had taken off for their European destinations, the first waves were returning. This brought the sounds of fire engine bells, with firemen racing to help the bomber crews who had crash landed in their stricken bombers due to battle damage. Little wonder I suppose, that I now have trouble sleeping if it is too quiet.

My father had a good job in a reserved occupation at RAE Farnborough, having worked at Glosters for about 10 years. It was of course a very hard time during the war with rationing and extra demands on peoples time. He worked long hours at the airfield and then was often out all night on fireguard duty as well. He always told me that although the TV programme Dad's Army was funny, it was also very true to life!

My mother baked cakes and made clothes and did a lot of knitting to spread the pennies further. But many of her sporting pursuits were frowned upon for women to take part in in those days. So strong was the feeling that my father was told that if she persisted in pistol shooting, he could look for another job as the MoD didn't think it befitted a lady. I think she was always disappointed that I was a boy because she clothed me in dresses and kept my hair long until I started school. Even when I started school I still had to swap my shorts for dresses to please my mother when I came home from school. I of course, had to comply.

My father never drove a car, except for a brief spell on an `L` licence. Although he was very intelligent, having gained AMI Mech E, degrees and other qualifications, he was never very good at co-ordinating his hands and feet at the same time, hence he couldn't drive very well! My mother on the other hand, had a driving licence from the age of 14, and drove our 1932 Austin 7, which they bought new. My earliest recollections of the car were of her being blocked up with wooden blocks under the axles to keep the wheels off the ground during the war, because there was no petrol. My father tinkered about with it and kept it running, but I don't think it was on the road again until about 1947.

My mother was also mad on cards and would always be out at whist drives or bridge sessions. I expect you have now spotted where all this is leading. Both my parents were very busy, so I was farmed out a great deal to my father's mother, Gran Cally, who ran public houses in Aldershot. She had lived and worked in The Prince of Wales and managed two other pubs as well. She did this at first with my grandfather until he died and then became the first woman in the area to run pubs single handedly. In those days it was very rare for a woman to be a licensee of a pub and she ran three! She was Irish and had a hot temper like my father, but was generally all right to me. She was the spitting image of that well-known character in the Daily Express newspaper, `Grandma Giles' to look at, a barrel of a woman, 5 foot nothing high and always with the same little black rimmed hat on her head.

Sunday dinner times were always a pretty horrendous experience in the pubs in Aldershot at closing time. The children would come for their fathers, mostly soldiers, saying "mother wanted them home for dinner." Most of them were too far gone to bother about eating and there would be numerous punch ups with the children crying, whilst Gran Cally, small though she was, would efficiently set about the task of throwing some very large soldiers out of the door onto the pavement. No mean feat I thought. I was never a strong boy physically and I always marvelled at the way she accomplished these acts. It was amazing how quickly the military police were on the scene and no one argued with them.

Before I was 5 years old, I can remember that I never had a good appetite for food and was always crying at meal times, because I was being shouted at by my parents to eat more. I was often sick, because I was afraid my father would hit me. So I tried to force the food down even if I didn't want it or like it. I was never offered the choice of liking it or not, as food was still rationed and in short supply. I grew up knowing that I must eat anything that was put in front of me. I was never allowed to speak at the table, as it was considered rude and I was brought up purely on 'the child must be seen and not heard' principle. Sadly this attitude also seemed to exist away from the table as neither of them wanted to listen to me at any time. I always seemed to be just a nuisance and in the way. That probably contributes to the fact that I was always a loner at heart and very shy at school. This continued on right through my adult life until I was 46 years old when finally my life took a turn for the better.

However, though I had troubles eating, I quickly made up the calories by drinking alcohol secretly at my grandmothers pub. At the tender age of 5 years old I had mastered how to get cider from the barrels in the cellar and to this day I have never looked back. I remember one time not long after I had started school, I had stayed at Gran Cally's pub for the weekend. On Monday morning my mother couldn't wake me properly and thought I was ill. After trying hard to get me to school, she got most annoyed and took me to the doctor. She was annoyed because she couldn't go to London to shop as planned. When we saw the doctor, the diagnosis was that I was drunk! She went mad and dragged me home and gave me such a thrashing that I was bruised all over. So much so that she kept me off school for a couple of days until I could move properly again. It wouldn't have occurred to her that I might not understand about such things at that age. I did hurt, but I don't think it was much worse than going to school, which I didn't like right from the start. That was the first real thrashing that I remember and little did I know that it was to become a way of life.

I can't remember having any real friends at school and I didn't like parties, so I didn't meet many other children or people that I could relate to in any meaningful way. My parents didn't seem to tell me much and on the few occasions that I did ask questions I was usually made to feel a fool and told I was stupid or thick. So it was better just to keep quiet.

Having colds and visits to the doctor seemed to be regular occurrences. I was always under weight for my age and that seemed to worry my mother a lot. I apparently didn't eat as much as I should even when I was older and I remember that when the rationing was over, the doctor said I must eat at least one Mars bar a day along with my other food. I thought that was great as I wouldn't normally be given such treats, but my weight still didn't increase as it should. This problem I suspect is partly to blame for me always feeling that I must be the original 7 stone weakling who was a well known cartoon character during my formative years. This character was always displayed as a very thin gangling boy, portrayed in his swimming costume, being held down on a beach by other children and having sand kicked in his face by girls, the ultimate humiliation for a boy. Unfortunately for me, this came sadly true in later years and is why I never really felt that I was a man even when in my twenties and beyond.

Before starting school, one painful memory I do have is of a summer afternoon when I was riding my little 3 wheeled tricycle down a slope at the top of our garden in Farnborough. I used to drag my tricycle up to the top and get on it and free wheel down the slope. On this occasion I went too fast and went straight over the top of the handlebars. On the way through the air I felt such a pain somewhere between my legs as part of me had caught on the bell push handle as I went over the handlebars. My parents thought that pants for me were a waste of money so, as I only had a dress on, I didn't have any protection in a very vulnerable area. My mother came running out and pulled my dress up while I lay on the grass and she looked horrified, but I hadn't been able to look. She ran inside and got some bandage and came out and bound it around my 'willy' as I called it then and we got straight in the car and drove to the old Farnborough hospital, which has long since closed. Apparently my 'willy' had been cut from top to bottom and it was quite serious. While the doctor was stitching me up I remember my mother asking him if it would effect some function or other that I would be needing to perform in later life. I remember him saying that I would be able to perform quite normally and she needn't worry. Of course I didn't know at that age what they were talking about. But I have since wondered whether that accident or its repair had anything to do with the troubles which I had in later life. I do remember that it was painful for a long time and it was ages before I wanted to ride my tricycle again.

One other time that sticks in my mind was when I went into hospital to have my tonsils out as was fairly standard practice for children in those days. It was near Christmas and before my parents could take me home it snowed hard and the roads were impassable, so I had to stay in over

Christmas. It must have been the first time I had been away from my parents for so long. I remember the nurses and everyone being so concerned and kind at me being away from home, but it didn't bother me at all! I really enjoyed it and had a job handling all the attention and presents I was given as the warmth of the staff flowed over me like rivers of love. I had never known that feeling before. Lying in bed in a sort of frock like garment and walking about in it and not feeling cold was bliss. I was there for 10 days before my mother could come and pick me up in the car. It was easily the best Christmas of my childhood and I really didn't want to go home to my freezing cold house, or my parents.

I was always cold at home in the winter. There was no central heating then of course and just the old range for heating and cooking in the kitchen. I could never get to sleep as my feet were so cold and for most of my childhood I suffered with chilblains quite badly, as did my parents. I had to spend time and energy rubbing my feet with my hands most winter nights, to try and get them warm before I could sleep. I remember the cotton sheets being so cold and I never had pyjamas because my father didn't believe in them for me. He said that my body warmth would be wasted in heating the pyjamas instead of the bed! With hindsight I now feel that being a sickly child and in poor health a lot of the time, this could have been attributed to the damp houses and beds I used to sleep in. Also my mother used to tuck the blankets so tightly under the bed that there was always a very draughty gap either side of me. I wasn't strong enough to tug them loose to wrap round my neck more snugly. I also didn't dare get into trouble for undoing something that she had done for me.

My father, having completed his apprenticeship in Farnborough, then working for Gloster Aircraft Co near Cheltenham and returned to Farnborough. He then alternated between the two for most of his working life depending on who paid the most money. Our houses were always cold, damp, rented accommodation. More years than not, I can remember my bedroom windows being iced over from November to March, with the temperatures well below freezing in my bedroom for most of that period. I dreaded the winter because my colds and bad chests seemed to go on forever and the various medicines didn't appear to do any good for me. But my parents never kept me off school if I wasn't well as this would have interrupted their lives too much. They were not happy on the times when I was brought home by a teacher from school because I was obviously ill and couldn't cope.

By the age of 5 or 6, I was often called 'spineless', 'weak' or 'dummy' by my parents and I'm afraid the phrases got worse as I got older and were frequently used at home and also at school. I seemed to be put down all the time and any enthusiasm I had for anything as a child was soon squashed and I believed that I was no good in the end and my spirit was crushed. I didn't bother about learning or doing things right, because whatever I tried to do was criticised as being no good or hopeless. On the other hand no one told me how to do things right. I know it seems stupid now but I was too scared to ask my parents or teachers as no one was interested in helping me anyway.

It so encourages me now when I see my godsons asking their parents questions and being listened to, given the time that they need to learn something and encouraged to ask questions when they don't understand things. As a result they have good self-esteem and have a sense of belonging to a family which brings them security and confidence, none of which I can ever remember feeling at home or school. Small wonder I suppose, that I soon got labelled as a no hoper, a troublemaker and I suppose in today's language, a wimp. Children were generally not encouraged to question things in those days as they do now, so I just thought that these feelings of inadequacy were normal. I only found out years later that it didn't need to be like that.

CHAPTER 2

<u>Boyhood Bewilderment</u>

I didn't last long at my first school in Farnborough. My parents were summoned to the school one day and told by the headmaster that I had stolen another boy's pen, which was found in my satchel. This boy had never liked me and used to bully me and had obviously framed me by putting the pen there himself, or forcing someone else to do it. I don't think this first offence would be grounds for expelling a pupil today, but my parents were furious that their son should be expelled from his first school just before his 7th birthday. I did try and tell them and the headmaster that I hadn't done it, but to no avail, so I had a bad start at school life.

When we got home I was really frightened. I was banished to my bedroom and given a good talking to by my father and was left in no doubt that the punishment next time would be far worse than I was going to receive this time. He then stripped me of all my clothes, even my socks, and twisted my right arm up behind my back with my hand right up behind my neck. This really hurt me and I thought that that was my punishment, but not so. He made me kneel by the side of the bed and forced my chest down on to it and with my wooden school ruler he whacked my buttocks and top part of my legs.

I was petrified and screamed, but he said if I didn't be quiet I would receive worse treatment, so I just cried and cried. He then took the clothes off the bed, luckily it was summer, and told me to stay on the bare mattress until morning. I think this was about 5pm and I'd only had a sandwich at school for lunch, but I didn't get any more food or drink until breakfast next morning.

I think that was the first time I ever felt really frightened of my father at home. I felt so helpless and began to wonder if I really was that bad. My father had gone to work by the time my mother came to get me up, and although it was summer, I could never remember being quite so cold before. I couldn't move for a while and my mother rubbed me with her hands to get my joints moving again. I thought she was being kind but looking back, I do wonder why she didn't come to find me the night before and make sure I was alright. My right shoulder felt as if it was on fire and my behind and legs hurt terribly. In fact my legs were quite weak and I had a job to walk at first. I think my mother thought I was putting it on, but I really wasn't. I just ached all over, as if all the stuffing had been knocked out of me, which it had.

My body was still hurting a couple of days later when it was my 7th birthday. I remember I received a dinky toy double-decker bus and my mother said I was lucky to get that, because my father thought I only deserved a card after I'd humiliated him at school. She said she had to have an argument with him to get that bus for me.

They then took me to Gran Cally's pub in Aldershot quite early that morning while my father tried to sort out another school for me. I was so relieved to be with her instead of at home because I usually had a good time with her. I was so pleased with my double-decker bus that I didn't let it out of my sight for days.

I had more presents from Gran Cally; sweets and cakes which she had made (and cider!) and in the event I stayed with her for a few nights which I was so grateful for. She rubbed some soothing cream on my wounds as well, though no questions were asked. I was just about healed by the time my parents took me home and I was very sad to leave her.

When I got home my father gave me another lecture and made me promise that I would never steal again from anyone. For a while I continued to plead my innocence, but he was getting more and more angry and I didn't want another thrashing, so I gave in and promised him I wouldn't steal again. This pattern became the story of my life, accepting the blame and giving in all the time, in an attempt to avoid more punishment.

My father said he had booked me into another school in Farnborough and we had to go and see the headmaster that afternoon. This we did and the headmaster managed to frighten me to death on the first visit! I was told what was expected of me and what wouldn't be tolerated. He also said he was very keen for all pupils to compete in as many sports as possible. The school had a very high standing when competing in southern area championships and he expected me to carry the school colours with honour.

This was all I wanted to hear as I didn't like football or any sport much at that age. I think it was mainly because of my puny figure. My body was so thin and weak that I didn't like showing any more of it than I had to and I seemed to be feeling even more self conscious than ever after my father had stripped me and left me overnight. I was very shy. I remember keeping long sleeved shirts and pullovers on even in the summer so I didn't show my puny arms. My legs were very thin as well and I was always falling over and cutting my knees. I longed for long trousers from a very early age, but they weren't worn by children then until they were quite old, so I had to suffer my thoughts alone. Having been frightened by the headmaster right from the first meeting, I wasn't at all looking forward to starting at his school the following week.

I made the most of my few days grace and went to my Gran Cally again because my father went abroad with his work and my mother had all her hobbies lined up and a 3-day cricket match. I was beginning to enjoy life, away from my parents. It was so much better than being at home.

Starting another school was quite nerve racking for me and my first impressions were that a lot of the girls and boys seemed very rough, especially at play time. I wished my mother or someone had taken me on that first day, because I felt quite scared of the unknown. My mother walked me up to the bus and saw me onto it and then I felt so alone. When I arrived at the school I was ushered into the morning assembly by my teacher and was relieved that she seemed a bit better than the headmaster. We stood all the time and had some hymns and a reading before entering class.

The school took children right from 5 to leaving age, which in those days was 15. This surprised me because the building didn't look very big. The desks were attached to wooden benches which were so hard to sit on all day long. We had ink wells and pens with nibs in those days and I found it all very messy. I got ink on my shirt on the first day so I was in trouble when I got home.

I will always remember my first school play time in the morning at that school. I had butterflies in my tummy so I thought I wanted to go to the toilet. They were all outside in those days and I'd just found an empty one and was just sitting down, when a big boy clambered over the top of the locked door. He unlocked it, opened it, and there was a gang of older boys and girls, not from my class, staring at me.

The school was surrounded by large cast iron railings about 6ft high, with the vertical rails spaced about 6 inches apart. These children then told me they would like to give me the "traditional" welcome to the school. They then dragged me outside, still with my trousers round my ankles, I never wore any pants or vests so I felt very exposed and humiliated. My arms were then twisted behind and through the railings, with my back pulled tight against them. I was then punched in the stomach once by every member of the gang, about 8 or 10 I think. I had no idea what I had done to deserve this. Where were the teachers? It was all over very quickly and they ran off and I was left sliding down the railings trying to extricate my arms. I felt very weak because I don't think I had ever been punched in my stomach before. Another boy who I didn't know then, came and helped me up and pulled my trousers up. His name was Alan, and that was the first of many times that he thankfully came to my aid. Then the bell went to end playtime and we split up and went to our various classes.

I sat down in class in a daze, really trying to think what I had done to be treated like that. Also the thought that girls as well as boys could hurt anyone in that way, completely unprovoked, was totally bewildering to me. Then I was suddenly aware of the teacher's face in front of me and her mouth moving but I hadn't heard a thing. The next thing I knew I was hauled out of my desk and stood in front of the class in a corner facing the wall. The teacher told me if I made a noise or moved, I would be sent to the headmaster. My legs were like jelly and tears were running down my cheeks, wetting my shirt. But I had learned to keep quiet at times like this. What a start for my first day!

She left me there until the end of the class and then it was home time. I walked out of the school gates wishing I never had to return there. I was still shaking when I stood at the bus stop and got some funny looks and comments from some other children. Going home on the bus I wondered whether I should say anything to my mother when I got in. When I arrived she was engrossed in painting a wall and although she did ask me how I got on, she wasn't really listening, so I didn't say anything. I went to my room and worried about what was going to happen the next day.

We had tea and my father asked me how my first day went. I remember starting off by saying I didn't like the school dinner, especially the pudding which was the first of what was to be many of figs and prunes. I didn't like them then and I still don't. I always remember it was a job to get in the toilets at school after that pudding, as it had the same effect on all of us and they were all full up! However I got no sympathy from my parents and my father said he was paying good money for my school dinners and I was to get used to them and eat them all up. I could see he wasn't very happy so I didn't have the courage to mention the bullying or the confusion of being made to stand in front of the class. I just hadn't heard what the teacher had said to me, as I was in such a state after that break time that I couldn't focus on anything.

After tea I went outside to catch the last of the early autumn evening sun. I have always found the hot sun to be so soothing and relaxing and I sorely needed both of those.

I have always loved sunbathing, like my mother, but on this occasion I just couldn't relax and felt very tense. I lay there on the grass thinking that my second school was no better than the first. I then went to bed feeling utterly dejected and alone and not wanting to wake up for school the next day. I cried myself to sleep, but it was very fitful sleep and I woke many times dreading the time I would have to get up and face the day ahead.

People say that tomorrow never comes and I never understood that as a boy, because it always seemed to come too soon for me. As usual I opted out of telling the teacher of my treatment in the playground, mainly I think because as the torturers left me, they said that if I told anyone I would really get hurt. Being an only child I had not experienced this sort of treatment before and I was very scared. Maybe if I had had a brother or sister or both I might have had to stand up for myself before this. But I just had no experience of even playful rough and tumble and had no idea how to handle it at all. My stomach and lower ribs still hurt the next day from the punches when I breathed in, so I really didn't want any more of that treatment ever again.

The playground, with no teachers around, was just a battleground for many fights between the children and it was out of sight of the staff room of course. My time at that school was dogged with being picked on for fights in the playground, and smacks or canings from the teachers or the headmaster. I never won a fight and in the end I just never tried, because it was always me against many of them. Why was I always picked on I asked myself? Why me? I never did come up with the answer. It didn't help that the headmaster was mad keen on boxing. He would organise boxing sessions for the boys during our physical training lessons. He had an area roped off in the main hall that represented the size of a boxing ring. He split us off into pairs who would then fight each other over three rounds, each of three minutes duration. There were only two pairs of boxing gloves which had to be removed from the previous contestants before my bout could begin. Of course they never fitted and there was no protective head gear so we all had bloody noses soon after the start of our first round. I used to get knocked down very early on and seemed to spend most of the first round trying to regain my feet until the headmaster, who was also the referee, reluctantly stopped the fight in favour of my opponent. As I said before I never won a fight and often ended up banished to the headmasters office for the cane because I hadn't tried hard enough. I will always remember how humiliated I felt in front of the other children and I'm sure that those situations continued to crush any remaining spirit I had left within me.

One of the reasons for the amount of brutality at the school could have been that there weren't many civilian children at the school, as we had many children from the army families in Aldershot. I suppose my class had about 60 pupils, which was not unusual for those days. This was split about 12 civilian, 27 army and 21 gypsy or tinkers. These groups mainly stuck together and the fights were mainly between the groups. The army and gypsy children all seemed very rough to me and I got a lot of stick from them because I didn't fit into any of the groups. They always roamed about in gangs and I could never understand why they did that as I had always been on my own and mostly made my own amusement. Unfortunately my idea of amusement and playing for fun was very different to theirs. It always amazed me that the gypsies and tinkers were always feuding because I thought they were rather similar.

I just wanted plain happiness for myself and others, and I couldn't understand why these children, especially when they got together, seemed to get their pleasure by mentally and physically hurting others. The boys, and even the girls in my class, always seemed stronger than me and I felt so humiliated when held captive by one particular girl. She would hold my arms twisted up behind my back while her mates groped my testicles and penis in front of the other children. I also dreaded those iron school railings because of the many times I was held against them, frequently punched and sometimes worse. I never saw other children being treated this way, it was just me. Did I have "VICTIM" tattooed on my forehead or what? Maybe it was because they belonged to gangs who would stick up for them, but I had no one on my side. I also never understood why my penis was such a focus of their attention. I had no sex education at all. My parents made it quite clear to me that there were certain things that were not done or talked about and in those days the subject wasn't taught in school either. So I had no idea what the kids were doing to me and I couldn't talk to anyone about it as it was all taboo.

Looking back now, it comes as quite a shock to think that my father actually wanted to become a church minister. I really don't think he understood anything about love, certainly not where his son was concerned. But the family couldn't afford the training so he had to get a job to help support his mother as my grandfather had died so young at 45. I suppose his interest in the church was why I had to go to Sunday school at Farnborough parish church on Sunday afternoons which I hated. I must admit to bunking off more than I attended as it was so boring.

At all events, school or church, I grew up with some very fixed ideas constantly being hammered into my head. The wrath of God was taught at church and school and I knew only too well what the wrath of my earthly father was like, so I was certainly not drawn to learning any more about my heavenly one! My mother wasn't at all interested in the church. She always said that there were far better people who had never set foot inside a church and I was inclined to agree with her, if my father was anything to go by. I found it easy to understand why stealing, cruelty and deceitfulness were sinful, because they hurt other people. However by being made to go to Sunday school I began to realise that the mere act of worshipping, or at least attending a place of worship, is not in itself an indication of being a Christian. Yet one belief grew strongly in my mind, even then. That there is a greater power that shapes all our lives, past, present and future. Though at this stage I had no real understanding of what it was.

I suppose looking back, it's not surprising that my education suffered. I was always worrying about what was going to happen to me in the playground, on the way home or at home, instead of concentrating in class. My parents were very displeased with my reports and always went to the school to see what the matter was. It was not easy, but I did tell my parents of the bullying and my father said that the headmaster said I was a lying troublemaker who would not pay attention in class. So I then got a whacking from his hands which were very rough on my bare bottom. He said I was thick, idle and spineless and that any son of his should be able to look after himself. Then I would be banished to my bedroom sometimes with no tea and I felt so crushed and alone.

I was always in trouble when having classes of PT or games which I loathed. I hated undressing as all the other boys seemed to be much better built than me and stronger, and they wore pants. This may not sound like much of a problem now, but for me then, in the changing rooms, it often left me completely and unnecessarily naked. I would do almost anything to get out of these lessons, from forgetting my plimsolls to playing truant. I would much rather report to the headmaster for the cane, than participate in more humiliation at the hands of the PT teacher.

In the main hall we had frames with bars, ropes and things on them, which folded back onto the wall when not in use. We were supposed to climb these ropes and do pull-ups on the bars, which I could never do. I was usually made a laughing stock when my teacher singled me out to do these things in front of the class. I hated those frames because although I did try hard to do these exercises, I just couldn't do them. I was told to hang by one arm until I dropped and then the other one and so on by my teacher who said it would strengthen me. My arms and shoulders and hands hurt for days afterwards and on some occasions my shorts would be pulled down by the teacher leaving me hanging there starkers and feeling even more humiliated.

Imagine my relief when I heard my parents talking that there was a move afoot as my father had got a job at Gloster Aircraft Company, which was between Gloucester and Cheltenham. So I was then just trying to get through those tortures until I left that horrible school. About the only good thing I can remember about this school at the time, was that we were taken swimming once a week. There can't have been many large indoor swimming pools in the whole country in 1948, but the army had a lovely one near North Camp. It was called the Command Baths and was only about half a mile from the school. We were allowed to use it with the army's permission and each class went at different times. The teachers herded us into ranks and we were marched along the Queens Avenue to the pool, rain or shine.

It was an awe inspiring venue and the pool had a large deep end where the diving boards were situated. All the walking area at the pool sides were of marble and were very slippery. The changing cubicles and showers were also marble. The showers could be regulated by a lever to whatever heat one required and I used to stay in them for as long as possible. As I have said I hated undressing, but this pool had separate cubicles for changing, which alleviated my problem some what. The girls had their own showers so I was safe from them. There were no lockers and I used to leave my clothes and get into the water quickly if I could, before anyone saw my puny body. Even though it was heated I got cold quicker than most of the other children and didn't want to stay in as long as them.

I couldn't swim to start with, but I wasn't the only one thank goodness, so I didn't feel too bad about it. I loved the water, but I didn't like the swimming teacher or the fact that many children were learning to swim before me. Of course this was duly reported to my parents who weren't at all happy. Fortunately my mother belonged to the RAE Sports Club where my father worked and they were allowed into the pool on Sunday mornings. My mother liked swimming and it wasn't until she started teaching me that I began to learn the breast stroke properly, instead of doggie paddle. She was a good teacher and I soon learned to swim with her. I think these times together enabled us to have a greater understanding of each other and our relationship seemed to grow a bit closer over this period. She seemed so much more relaxed when my father wasn't present. I upset her sometimes when I got cold and wanted to get out before she was ready, but I so loved those hot showers, as I had never experienced anything like them before, they were bliss! There were no hot showers in homes in those days.

Also the little things, like my mother drying me with the towel after the shower, I used to look forward to, because I never got such attention at home. With her tuition my swimming soon improved and although I wasn't as strong or as fast as others in my class, there were many worse than me and at least I could swim! That did encourage me for a change, as I was usually one of the last to learn anything. Perhaps that was because the teacher couldn't give me as much attention as I needed, even if he was willing to, as there were 60 others in the class. So for once, my mother actually taught me something useful.

The only other times I seemed to get much attention from my mother was when I had nits in my hair. They seemed to be rife at school, especially amongst the gypsy children. Our hair was covered in a white powder by a teacher and then made to go and wash it off in cold water. I'm sure I caught a lot of my colds by having that done to me so often in the winter as we were not given towels to dry with, just left cold and wet. Thankfully my mother did it most of the time so I didn't have to have it done at school. She wasn't so rough with me as they were at school and I got my hair dried with a nice towel instead of it being left wet.

Another nightmare was when the school dentist came. My front teeth stuck out like rabbit's teeth and I had to wear a brace. This amounted to what looked like a very thick rubber band which was stretched over my two front teeth. This was supposed to pull them together and draw them back. It was very painful and I was always dribbling especially in bed. I wore it for many months but it didn't move my teeth at all, so it was a load of extra pain for nothing.

At last I knew the time was getting near for our house move because my mother was busy every day packing things into cases, boxes and anything she could get her hands on. My father was in Cheltenham sorting the other house out. The contracts were exchanged on a bitterly cold day in November with a heavy frost. We loaded the Austin 7 up with the last bits of luggage after the lorry had left with the furniture. The car was bursting at the seams. As it was so cold my father had run the radiator water out the night before because there was no anti-freeze in those days. So the last thing to do was to fill up the radiator before cranking the engine with the starting handle, which was permanently fixed to the engine shaft at the front of the car. This could be a warm job even on a cold day! There were two levers on the steering wheel for advancing or retarding the ignition and these had to be played about with until the correct position was achieved depending on the weather and how cold it was. My mother would usually sit in the car and fiddle with these while my father cranked until the engine started. It could be quite hazardous because due to the compression in the engine, the starting handle could kick back at you and damage your hand and arm if you weren't gripping it properly. However the little engine always fired in the end and I don't think it ever let us down, whatever the weather.

There was just enough space in the car for me to squeeze into and once in, I couldn't move. My mother backed the car down the drive and my father closed the gates. I looked out of the window at the house and I wasn't at all sad to leave. We dropped the keys off at the estate agents and then began the long haul to Cheltenham and another chapter in my life. By now I was eight years old.

CHAPTER 3

<u>Formative Years</u>

The drive to Cheltenham was a long, long haul and I felt very cold in the back of the car. I was hardly able to move until we stopped for a sandwich lunch and hot tea from our thermos flasks by the riverside at Pangbourne, near Reading. Although we had only done about 20 miles it was very slow going with the car all loaded up and the roads were twisty and narrow. At least it gave us a chance for a walk by the river to stretch our legs and the sun was warming us up nicely. There was no heating in the car as such but when the engine was running the heat did come through the bulkhead between the engine and the cab. In the summer it could be so intense that one could fry an egg on the accelerator pedal. For that reason, thick soled shoes were essential to drive this car and even then my mother had a block of wood positioned between her right foot and the accelerator pedal to stop it burning her foot!

We duly set off on the next leg of the journey through Wantage and Cricklade and this was very slow as we crawled up the Cotswold hills, in 1st gear a lot of the time with the car's wheels barely turning. We stopped at Cirencester on the top of the lovely Cotswold hills for more sandwiches, cake and flasks of tea. I've always disliked sitting down for long periods, especially on hard seats. I have never understood how people manage it. They must have a lot more padding on their behinds than I have, that is all I can think!

There was snow on the Cotswolds already. It could be such a wild place, but so beautiful too. Off we set on the last lap of our journey from Cirencester to Cheltenham. This was the highest part of the journey and it got colder as the sun went down with a lovely sunset of red, yellow and orange. This was an old Roman road and it could be very dangerous trying to pass anything because the dips in the straight road obscured oncoming vehicles. The acceleration on the car was not good as the body was heavy for the engine size and we were fully loaded. The view in front could look clear but one couldn't see if anything was in the dips. The headlights were not very bright either so it's just as well the car probably only had a top speed of about 50 miles an hour, wind assisted and down hill. We eventually crawled along to Birdlip Hill where the Cotswolds end in a sharp drop down a long steep hill into Cheltenham. My father thought it too steep for the fully loaded Austin 7 so we carried on to the Air Balloon pub and drove down Leckhampton Hill in low gear because although it was longer, it was less steep than Birdlip Hill.

The house my father was renting was not far from Leckhampton station, which was handy for travelling if we didn't have the car for any reason. It was an end of terrace property, two up and two down. One of the downs was a scullery and kitchen area with a great big stone sink and it all looked cold and uninviting to me. There was a large range in the living room with ovens on either side, which were very greasy. My father showed me to my bedroom which was quite small, about 10ft by 8ft I think, with a lath and plaster ceiling. In fact it was mostly laths and no plaster; I could see the sky through some of the slates and it didn't look very homely at all.

I helped to unload the car and it was getting late and cold and the removal men had left a lot of the furniture outside. My father thought he'd get on better if I was out of the way so my mother drove me round to her mother's. At this stage in my life I didn't know Gran Cook as much as Gran Cally because we only saw her sometimes for Easter or Christmas and perhaps for short stays in the summer. I had always liked her but I didn't know what she thought of me. Little did I know that she was to become my main anchor and such an important ally in the family.

Gran Cook was quite tall and thin like my mother was when she was young (whereas Gran Cally was short and round.) Gran Cook was always busy, but no matter what she was doing I always got a warm welcome and she stopped what she was doing to hug and kiss me. I wasn't used to this as my parents didn't deem it necessary, but I did enjoy it so. I felt so special for a change. My mother asked her if she could have me over the weekend until Monday morning, when Gran Cook would have to go to her cleaning job in Cheltenham during the week.

She always seemed very poor to me and only had the bare necessities in the house and for living. I didn't understand this as she was still working and I don't think my parents did either. I know my parents bought most of her coal for her because she couldn't afford it. Her little house was an end of terrace like ours that she rented, though it was in an even worse state of repair than ours. It had an identical great big black range, which was coal fired and with ovens on either side. I remember she used to spend ages cleaning and blacking the range and the hearth. She loved it to be spick and span at all times (quite unlike the house I had just moved in to), and she cleaned right through her house more than once a week. Everything had to be moved and all the chairs went on top of a big heavy dining table. I used to help her and I quite liked it because if I did things wrong she didn't scold me or hit me like my parents did. She just held my hand and told me how to do it right and showed me as well. Also I used to get sweets and chocolate as she would save them for me from her ration book. Things like sweets were still rationed until 1953 so this was a real treat.

Another time consuming job I remember her doing was curling her hair with a pair of tongs which she would heat up in the coals in the range. She would get a lock of hair together, catching hold of it at the ends between those tongs and rolled the hair up by rotating the tongs and somehow the heat made the hair stay in a curl. Then another lock was gathered and so on until all the hair was curled and it took ages. I never knew why her hair never caught fire as there was plenty of smoke sometimes. Quite frightening I thought!

I think these were her three main pursuits at home and I know they were always a bone of contention between my parents and her. They used to want to take her out in the car thinking it would make a nice change for her but she very rarely went out with them because she either had the range, her 'er` (that is the way she said hair!) or the cleaning to do. She was very independent (or I thought she was) and I know she would rather go without coal and freeze, rather than have it bought for her by my parents. But they usually ordered it and had it delivered anyway, so she had no say in it!

There was one big old comfortable armchair close to the range, which was always occupied by Smutter, the cat. He was a lovely big, long-haired moggy and I think he thought the chair was his. I often struggled to tip him off the chair, and he was always back in it before I could get there. He was so affectionate and never scratched and was always put out at night. I could never get anywhere near the house without being greeted by Smutter well down the unmade lane. If we were in the car he would spot us from even further away. He was quite old but nothing was on his territory for long, he would see anything off, cats or dogs! I believe that the term used for soot in that area was smut, and as he was as black as soot, Smutter was a good choice of name for him.

Another resident in Gran Cook's home was a large, beautifully coloured jay bird. This was Gran's pride and joy and lived in a metal cage which was about four feet square. It must have had a strong beak because I noticed the bars of the cage were bent all over the place. I have never known a bird speak so clearly and it would pick up phrases it was taught very quickly. It spoke much clearer than any budgerigar I had ever heard and of course some people taught it swear words, which were quite frequently used, much to Gran Cook's embarrassment! When it died many years later, Gran Cook had it stuffed and it stood in a glass case on the sideboard for all to see.

Both our houses had outside toilets, unlike the house at Farnborough which had an inside bathroom. I really suffered trying to use the toilet, sitting on that freezing seat in winter. I used to take newspaper to sit on but still I couldn't perform in the cold even when I needed to. The only good news was that in those days the print didn't come off when you wiped your bottom as it would these days!

I stayed with my Gran Cook all that weekend, and was very aware of my parents not being there. I felt so different somehow, as though a weight had been lifted off my shoulders and I think I was receiving a sense of relaxation for the first time. I wasn't used to getting as much attention as Gran Cook gave me and she actually asked me what I thought about things. I was struck dumb I'm afraid. I didn't know how to have any opinions as my views were not required at home. I was expected to do what I was told without question and that was it.

That turned out to be one of the best weekends of my childhood up to that time, even better than Christmases and holidays. I felt like I was someone for the first time in my life. I remember as she put me to bed on the first night she asked me where my pants and vest were. I told her I'd never had any or pyjamas either and she muttered something under her breath which I couldn't catch. She asked me if I felt cold and I said yes, so she found me a shirt which I put on and it came down to my knees. It was going to be a very heavy frost again that night, so she put me in her bed and went downstairs after hugs and kisses. I could hear her moving about downstairs while I was warming up under a big duck feather filled eiderdown and many blankets. I soon warmed up, even my feet warmed up quicker than usual. I wasn't used to all this comfort and luxury. At home I had to rub myself for hours sometimes to get warm and there were never as many clothes on the bed as I had now. It was bliss and I soon went into a deep sleep.

I awoke in the night needing the toilet. I was lying on my side and Gran Cook had one arm around me. I felt so warm and secure lying there with her. I carefully raised her arm so she didn't wake up and felt around under the bed for the `joey` which was always there to save going outside. It wasn't so easy to switch the lights on in those days because these were gas and the mantles always seemed to be damaged as they hung a bit low and people hit them with their heads. I found the joey, which was a china bowl with a handle. I kneeled down and weed into it trying to keep my long shirt out of the way, a bit difficult in the dark, but I managed. It was cold and I slipped back under the clothes and cuddled up to my grandmother. I felt so wanted and peaceful for a change and I soon fell asleep again.

When I awoke I was on my own in bed and didn't really want to get out into the cold. It sounded as though Gran Cook was stoking the range downstairs and I lay there thinking she must be the kindest person I had ever met. Soon after, she came up to tell me she was cooking breakfast. I always looked forward to her breakfasts of bacon (if she had any), egg, tomato and toast. She said I'd better start getting up and she sat on the side of the bed and gave me a kiss and cuddle. I then put my shorts, socks and shoes on and went downstairs, keeping my shirt on as long as possible in the cold. Gran Cook poured some hot water out of the battered old kettle into a tin bowl in the stone sink. I took my nightshirt off and she asked me if she should wash me, as it would be quicker. I liked that but it was nearly a bath. I was washed face, neck, ears, front and back, down to my waist! She rubbed me dry nice and briskly and I soon warmed up when I put my shirt and two jumpers on and sat by the range where our breakfast was cooking.

I warmed up even more when I had eaten my delicious breakfast. There was a thick frost outside and as always the radio wasn't working because the big, heavy accumulator (battery) had run out. This was before the days of batteries that we know now. When I had been there before with my father this was the first job I had been given, so I offered to take it down the village shop to get a replacement. She thought it was a bit heavy for me but my father hadn't bothered about that. She said I was good to offer and that she would come with me because she wanted some other things too.

I opened the door after wrapping up in my lumber jacket and gloves and Smutter sneaked in for his breakfast and went straight on to the chair by the range. I went round to the back garden and got the wheel-barrow, which was quite big for me to manage at 8 years old.

The wheel was frozen solid but I managed to free it after a struggle. I brought it round to the front door and we disconnected the accumulator and loaded it into the wheelbarrow and off we set for the shop. It was about a mile along mostly unmade lanes and was very slippery. The barrow was quite heavy for me, but I liked to help Gran, although she pushed it more than I did. The sun was up now and the frost was melting off the trees. It was a lovely day really, although I've always liked warm weather best. The sky was a clear deep blue, the birds were singing and various animals were scuttling about in the hedgerows as we frightened them, clattering along with the barrow. I felt so happy and so safe with Gran Cook. Why couldn't life always be like this I thought?

We finally arrived and Gran Cook did some other shopping first. The shopkeeper was cheery and he recognised me. He said he would put the exchange accumulator in the barrow while we shopped. We went to the grocers and paper shop so that Gran could find out what was showing at the cinema, though she never actually bought a paper! Best of all, we went into the sweet shop where she used her hard earned money on me instead. I was never all that fond of sweets, but I did like Mars bars and she bought me one to eat on the way back.

The accumulator was all ready when we got back to the shop, but there was only one snag, Gran hadn't got enough money. Not to worry, everyone knew each other and it was put on the slate for payment later. Off we went after saying our goodbyes and thanks to the shopkeeper on what I thought at that age was quite a long walk home. I had eaten my Mars bar by now and I was much warmer. Gran asked me if I would like to go to the cinema to see Snow White and the Seven Dwarfs in the afternoon and I jumped at it. I think that was one of the few things Gran Cook really enjoyed, going to the cinema. That was probably her one weakness. I remember my mother saying she couldn't understand why Gran went to see The King and I eight times!

We had got about half way home when Smutter appeared out of the hedgerows with rather a large vole in his mouth. He was made a fuss of by both of us before he sprang into the barrow for his free ride home, still not letting go of the vole! Gran Cook got us a quick dinner of bangers, mash and beans, home-made lardy cake and cups of tea and I felt really stuffed. Then we set off on another long walk to the cinema. There were three or four cinemas in Cheltenham at that time that I knew of and luckily it was the nearest one to Gran's place. But it was still at least a forty minute walk and I was glad to sink into the nice comfortable seats and have a rest when we got there.

This was quite an occasion for me, as I don't remember my parents taking me to the cinema before this. Though I used to walk along to the Saturday morning pictures that were put on for the children in those days and they were good. I thought the Snow White film was great and Gran loved it too. We had a great time. I came out with a bit of a stiff neck because we were quite near the front in the cheapest seats and I had to look up at quite an angle and off to one side, but it was really worthwhile. It was dark and cold when we came out but we were quite warm coming out of the cinema so didn't really feel it too much. Smutter met us about half a mile from home and got a fuss made of him. We went indoors and stoked the range with more coal and Gran Cook made us hot thick soup and did some crumpets and peanut butter which I seemed to live on. I loved peanut butter then and still do. I suppose I was brought up on it because it substituted for butter when butter was still rationed. We listened to the radio and Gran played Snakes and Ladders and Ludo with me and read me a story before going to bed. This never happened at home either. I did so enjoy my time with Gran Cook.

In between those games Gran took what looked like a long handled saucepan with a lid. It was brass I think, and she filled it with hot coals from the range. She then put it in the bed and every so often would go up and move it about. Just before I went to bed, I would put it where I thought my bottom would be and it was bliss when my bare behind touched those sheets. The bed was lovely, warm and comfortable and I slept with Gran again. I soon dropped off to sleep.

Sadly, all good things come to an end and my mother collected me the next day. I thanked Gran Cook ever so much for having me and treating me so well with all our outings and I climbed into the Austin 7 and waved goodbye with tears in my eyes. As we drove away I thought the only good thing was that at least we weren't going as far away as Farnborough and I hoped I would see Gran Cook more often now.

My father was waiting for us when we arrived home that morning and said that he had made an appointment for us to meet the headmaster at my new school in Cheltenham after dinner. I wasn't looking forward to that. I just hoped it would be better than my last school in Farnborough.

My parents had just about got the furniture and everything straight in the house and my bedroom looked a bit better now with the furniture in it, although I still couldn't see out of the windows for the ice. My mother got us some dinner and my father took me to the new school. It was within walking distance, about 20 minutes from home so he told me to remember the way. We had our chat with the headmaster, who didn't seem too bad. What I did notice was that the school building was very similar to my last one with those awful iron railings surrounding it and the torturous climbing frame with ropes that swung out from the wall in the main hall. Oh why couldn't the railings have been taken for the war effort I thought.

The school looked empty when we got there and the good news was that the outside toilets had frozen up so the children had all been sent home. This gave me a welcome breather to explore the area and in the event, I didn't start school for another week until they'd managed to thaw out the toilets. By now my father had started work and my mother was flying round joining all her clubs and organisations, so I had plenty of time to find the shops where I used to go to warm up! I was at home on my own most of the time and there was no heating except for the coal fire which I wasn't trusted to look after it so it wasn't lit. It was bitterly cold and I used to run around a lot to get warm. I was quite happy on my own because at least I wasn't being hurt or shouted at all the time.

I desperately wanted to be stronger in my body and I used some of this time to go into the surrounding woods. I found a tree with a horizontal branch at about the right height for me to hang from, so I could practice my pull-ups and strengthen my shoulders and biceps. Everyone else seemed to be able to do them so why couldn't I? What I hadn't thought about was that all the other children were off school as well and while I was trying to do pull ups, I was pounced on by a mixed gang of girls and boys who I had never seen before. I was terrified as they pulled me down and spread-eagled me on my back on the freezing muddy, leafy ground.

The boys held my wrists and ankles while the girls stripped me from the waist down. They then pinned me down and took it in turns to wee in my face, holding my nose to make my mouth stay open. With the boys it was a steady stream making me feel like I was going to drown. The girls sprayed all over my face and I was completely covered in it and stank. The wee in my eyes made them sting horribly and for what seemed like an age, I was completely unable to see. I was then forced into a sitting position while my lumber jacket, jumper and shirt were removed. They then produced a rope and I was stood up naked with even my shoes and socks removed and backed up to a tree, with my wrists being tied tightly behind the trunk. I thought I was going to die as the temperature couldn't have been much above freezing in those woods because the sun didn't penetrate the trees. I was called all sorts of nasty names and taunted about my thin weak body and the girls said that no girls would want to know a weakling like me. The boys punched me in the stomach and the girls tickled me and pulled my testicles and penis. They said I would never grow into a man because my penis didn't get bigger. I didn't know what they were talking about but they did hurt me pulling it about. I begged them to release me as I was so cold and was hurting so much around the testicles and from the stomach punching. But they carried on taunting me for a while longer and then the boy ring leader said they would let me go if I promised not to say anything about this to my parents or anyone else. Because if I did they would really hurt me next time. What could I do? I promised all they asked and I was untied and just sank to my knees in the mire crying, while the gang ran off laughing.

I tried to pull myself together and attempted to dress myself as quickly as possible but my arms and shoulders were hurting me so much. My clothes felt damp after being thrown on the wet ground, so I headed for a shop as fast as I could that I knew would be nice and warm so I could thaw out a bit. I think that was the first time I had been tied up and I wondered how other children could ever do that to me and why. I wasn't doing anything wrong, or interfering with them. I was only trying to strengthen my puny biceps! What kind of people hurt others for their own pleasure? I couldn't understand it and I was probably in a state of shock when I look back on it now. I just hoped this was the first and last time that something like this would happen to me. Also I hoped that those children, who probably ranged between 8 and 12 years old, would not be at my new school. Alas I was to be disappointed on both counts.

When I got home, my mother was back and was very angry at the state of my clothes which were very dirty and the shirt was ripped. She asked me how I had got in such a state, so I said I had fallen over in the woods and that I had accidentally ripped the shirt while putting it on. I was shivering and she told me to take my clothes off and stand in front of the range to warm up while she went to find more clothes for me. I did warm up in front of the range, naked, looking at my puny body in the large mirror on the opposite wall. I tried not to cry but my ribs and stomach hurt when I breathed and my penis was swollen and bruised. I just sank on to my knees in front of the range and my mother came down and asked me what was wrong. I couldn't tell her because she didn't really want to know anyway and she didn't notice the bruising. So she told me to stop that awful noise and put the clothes on that she'd got or I could go to my bedroom with no dinner. I managed to stop crying because I needed some food after my ordeal and I pleaded with her not to tell my father about it.

Luckily he was on overtime and I didn't see him before I got packed off to bed after having my dinner at 7.30 that evening. I couldn't eat much of my meat as it was tough and that didn't please my mother either. I didn't really like meat except for sausages because it always seemed tough and I never knew whether it was the meat or my mothers cooking of it. Thinking about it now, my teeth and gums were always painful and the school dentist never seemed to do anything about them, except for that brace which hurt even more and looked terrible as well. That could have been the problem with meat but no one seemed to listen to me. I was just making a fuss about nothing, as my parents would say. I got into bed and that was a freezing cold shock after the last couple of nights in my Gran's bed. I rubbed myself for ages trying to get warm even though so much of my body was sore. Of course I didn't have Gran Cook's shirt on now and I did so wish I was back with her.

As there was no school I didn't get up so early and when I came downstairs my mother was playing the piano. She played well. There didn't seem much that she couldn't do. After I'd washed and dressed and I was eating my porridge (the doctor had recommended it to fatten me up) she said that she and my father had decided that instead of idling my time away playing in the woods or going round the shops, I would be better employed learning the piano. I remember saying I would rather go out to play than learn the piano. She said I should not be so ungrateful as it cost a lot of money for lessons and lots of children would be so glad of the opportunity. I said I had enough trouble with school lessons without adding piano ones. She said I was talking rubbish and the decision had been made and that's all there was to it. She was going to see a teacher that day to book up my first lesson. I wasn't very enthusiastic which, of course, upset her. But I knew that just because she could play well, she would expect me to as well and I would get more hassle if I didn't live up to her expectations.

I duly started the lessons soon after with a lady called Miss Rudge, on a Saturday morning, which didn't please me at all. She lived in a bungalow not far from where we lived with her sister. Although I didn't like going there much at first, she was very nice to me and took me along very slowly with the teaching at first. Too slowly from my parents' point of view because they were paying good money and didn't seem to see any progress from scales for months. Miss Rudge said it was much better to know all the basics thoroughly before going on to other things and that meant singing in key as well, which I did enjoy.

Miss Rudge said that my parents wanted me to sit examination grades on the piano and that frightened me to death as I had never passed any exams at school. I thought that playing the piano for a hobby was different and having to take exams would spoil it. My father didn't think I was progressing very fast over the first 6 months, so he said I had to practice for at least one hour a day, except Saturday when I had the hours lesson. I wasn't happy with that of course, but what could I do? So I said that before I did an hour a day on it, I thought that the piano ought to be tuned, because it didn't sound anything like Miss Rudge's piano and it sounded like I was hitting the wrong notes when I wasn't. He nearly hit the roof and said if it was good enough for my mother it was good enough for me. I thought he was going to hit me but my mother luckily came in and asked what was going on. My father told her what I'd said and she actually agreed with me for a change and said that she had meant to have a word with him about getting it tuned before now. I was so relieved and slipped out of the room, while they finished their argument.

Miss Rudge had a proper grand piano, which was one of the best types and we had an old upright piano, which after so many moves must have needed attention anyway. My father did get it tuned and I watched the man do it. It was very interesting to hear him tell me what he was doing and what was wrong. The only trouble was that now I had to practice an hour a day, which I didn't relish at all. How could I enjoy something that I was forced into and it was another thing that I couldn't do well enough to please my parents.

CHAPTER 4

Adding Insults to Injuries

I started my new school on the Monday, and went into assembly in the big hall for hymns and a talk from the headmaster. I was introduced to my teacher, shown to my desk and to my horror I was placed right next to the ringleader of the girls that had recently humiliated me in the woods. She was the only one of the gang in my class, but I had noticed some of the other members at assembly. I had thought at the time they were older and so would be in a higher class. My heart sank and I couldn't concentrate on that first day at all. When I left at night, I noticed that a girl and boy from the gang followed me all the way home. I wasn't sure if they were following me to find out where I lived, or whether they lived in the same direction, but I was frightened.

When I got indoors there was no one at home, but the back door was unlocked. There were no fires lit so the temperature was down to about freezing inside. I thought I had better change out of my school clothes and into my old ones. While I was naked I saw myself in the mirror and I remember just standing there looking at my puny body and wondering who I was and what I was meant to be doing on this earth? Was this life what it was meant to be? Why should I be tormented by others all the time? To take my mind off it I thought I would do some exercises as it always felt much easier to do them whilst not restricted by any clothes. I used to do this quite often after school to try and get stronger.

Some time later while I was still doing my exercises both my parents came back and they were having an argument as usual. My mother was wanting more money for something. Shortly afterwards my father burst into my bedroom and found me stretched out on my back with my hands behind my head, doing my leg raises. he was furious and said why hadn't I pulled all the curtains and what was I doing? I said I was exercising my stomach muscles and he said I hadn't got any to exercise and that I was more likely playing with myself while they were out of the house. I didn't understand what he meant, I think I was still too young. He said if I had all this time on my hands I should have been practising the piano, to which I replied that my fingers were too cold. He went mad and told me not to answer him back and he grabbed my left arm and twisted my wrist up between my shoulder blades and threw me over his knee and spanked my bare behind until I screamed for mercy. He got up and I fell to the floor crying. "That will teach you to bare your bottom to me." He shouted. "Get your clothes on and get practising on that piano now" and he stormed out of my bedroom. I couldn't decide where I hurt most, my arm or my bottom. I had great trouble getting my arm down from being pressed between my shoulder blades and I looked in the mirror and my bottom was a mess of great purple wields.

I heard him shouting for me to get downstairs quick and start practising on the piano, so I quickly dressed and went down. Soon it was tea time and it passed in a deathly hush. No one was speaking to each other. I thought they might want to know how my first day at school went, but I wasn't asked and after tea I was told to go straight to bed for being such a filthy boy. I still didn't know what he was talking about, but I went to bed nursing my wounds and spent a long time rubbing my legs and feet trying to get them warm before I fell into a fitful sleep. I remember my mother coming in that night and picking me off the floor and putting me back in bed and telling me to stop shouting. So whether I had a nightmare or something I don't know, she didn't ask. But I eventually went back to sleep dreading school the next day.

My father woke me in the morning and told me to get in the bath, as he didn't want to waste the water he had used. Of course it was the old tin bath in the scullery in those days, and we had to heat the water on the range or the gas stove and it all cost money. By the time I got in the water it was pretty cold and dirty. I don't know how long it had been there, I shivered all over and it was difficult to wash myself properly because I ached and hurt from the previous night. Nobody was speaking at breakfast again and I made my way to school on a cold frosty morning, feeling very alone, cold and down hearted.

I had difficulty sitting on the hard wooden bench seats of the desk at school because my bottom hurt so much and I was wriggling about a bit. The teacher told me to stop a couple of times, but when she had to tell me the third time she hauled me out in front of the class. She made me print `wriggle bottom' on a piece of card in big letters and pinned it on my bottom. She then made me stand in a corner at the front of the class, facing the wall, with my hands clasped behind my head. This was so painful because my arms and shoulders hurt already from my father's treatment the night before. I couldn't hold the position for very long and started crying so the teacher paraded me up and down the class room telling the other pupils that this is what a weak, spineless, insubordinate trouble maker looked like and they all laughed at me. On the way home two boys and two girls taunted me and called me names, before twisting my now useless arms even more and running off when I screamed.

I couldn't face going home so I walked about 5 miles to Gran Cook's house. She could see I was in a state and asked me what had happened. She was so understanding, but said she would have to take me home because my parents would worry. I was frightened about what my father would say but she said not to worry, she would explain.

I was so tired when I got home and Gran made a good case for me bless her and I had some tea and went to bed. I could hardly move my arms the next morning and was in a lot of pain. My mother dressed me and took me to the doctors after breakfast. He asked me where I hurt and I said my arms and shoulders only, because my mother had told me not to mention my bottom. He asked me how it happened and I told him at school and coming home and he said he would write to the headmaster.

I had 2 weeks off school with my injuries and much of that time was spent with Gran, which was lovely. She really looked after me and even fed me on some occasions in the first week when I couldn't manage to feed myself. She took me to the pictures and had me in bed with her when I suffered really bad nightmares. The doctor had given a prescription to my mother for some ointment to rub into my arms and shoulders, which she did rather roughly. Gran Cook was so gentle when she was doing it, but I still had trouble trying not to cry.

I got to realise what a lovely person she was over those two short weeks and when the awful day came that I had to go back to school, I knew that if I had troubles there was one person in this rotten world that I would get a fair hearing from and that meant so much to me. It was a sort of lifeline and an anchor. I never did have any more trouble from that teacher, so perhaps the doctor's note did have the desired effect. Even though it was actually my father who had done most of the damage to me.

I wasn't getting on very well at school and was by now considered backward, having never finished higher than 44th in the class out of about 50. This didn't please my parents of course as they wanted to tell people how well I was doing and their Edward was going to do so well.

My father had a talk with the headmaster after one exam disaster and it was decided that I should have homework. I had this most days and weekends and my life at home became even more miserable and I got a lot of stick from my father when I couldn't get it right. He would stand over me for ages showing me how it should be done, but I still had difficulty following what he was saying. Besides the homework, I was still supposed to do my hour a day piano practice, so I didn't get much time to play or see Gran Cook as I used to, which made me very sad. There were two children up the road who I used to play with a bit, but I wasn't allowed to see them until I had practised the piano and done the homework and by then it was usually too late. I think this was a ploy by my parents as for some reason they didn't like the families of these two children, so didn't want me to play with them anyway. I never understood why because they were friendly towards me unlike most other children I had encountered. When we did manage to get together we never really did much except talk, but there was no physical contact at all which made me feel safe for a change.

When doing my homework I did try hard to get the answers right, but it was never good enough for my parents and finally at the end of a two hour session with my father one night, he exploded and said he just didn't understand how a son of his could be so thick. He marched me upstairs and told me to get undressed and then marched out of my bedroom. I thought he just meant for me to go to bed and it was cold, so I did. To my horror he came back with two pieces of rope and two of his old ties. He shouted at me to get up, whatever did I think I was doing? He was going to punish me for not getting my homework right and then perhaps I would pay more attention. "No son of mine is going to turn out to be a dunce" he said.

He told me to sit on the side of my bed and I was shaking with fear as he tied one of his ties to each of my wrists and the pieces of rope to each of my ankles and then I was thrown on my back on top of my bed. He pinned each bicep down with his knees whilst tying each wrist to the top corner posts of the bed. He was a big man and his knees bit into my bony arms and I was so frightened as to what he was going to do next. He then pulled the ankle ropes very tight to the bottom corner posts of the bed, so spread-eagling me. I could hardly breathe and my shoulders were on fire and I pleaded with him to let me go. But he said that if I didn't try harder at school and on the piano, this is just a small taste of what I can expect to correct me. Before he left me he tickled my armpits and feet and of course as I wriggled so I hurt even more. Finally he left and it hurt me even to cry so I just lay there cold and scared, wondering how long he would leave me. So many things went through my mind. I wanted Gran Cook and I wanted to run away. I was still only 8 years old.

It was about 2 hours before he finally released me and told me to go to bed and there would be no tea for me. I remember being so cold, but I hurt so much that I hadn't got the strength to rub myself warm. My shoulders and arms just wouldn't work. I hardly slept at all that night wondering that if he could do that to me for wrong homework answers, what more was he capable of? Being naked I had felt degraded, humiliated, so cold and utterly worthless. Unfortunately this seemed to be the pattern of my life at that age, but when I wasn't forced to do homework or piano practice, I would go to see Gran Cook for some love and consolation. She was so good to me and only she made my life worth living. I think she had some idea of what was going on at home, but in those days physical punishment was the norm. She knew what a temper my father had and that it would be no good trying to interfere on my behalf. But what she did do was to love me all the more while I was with her.

There was one time of the year that I did look forward to, and that was our annual holiday at Paignton in Devon. My mother loved the sun and swimming in the sea and I must take after her in that respect. My father was fair to ginger haired with fair skin and he burned easily and I don't think he would have gone on holiday at all if my mother hadn't pushed him so hard! They asked my Gran to come but she declined and I was so sad.

However I did look forward to the change of routine and my father seemed more relaxed when we were on holiday. We used to pile into the Austin 7 with all the luggage packed around me and I set off full of excitement at the prospect of two whole weeks at the seaside. We always stayed at the same hotel and booked a beach hut in more or less the same place. It was lovely to undress and go swimming from right on the sea front at Goodrington sands. It meant I could undress with no one seeing me in the hut and run down the sands and into the sea before I thought anyone could see my body. I enjoyed swimming, and I thought that if I really worked hard at it I would put on weight and get big muscles. But alas it never happened.

I loved sunbathing, but I was so self conscious of being thin that I rarely did it on the beach because too many people would see me. I would go behind the beach huts where there was a large park at Goodrington and try to find a spot on my own, where I wouldn't be seen.

The highlight of the whole holiday was when I was allowed to stay up later, just for one night, to see the firework display. Our holiday was always booked to coincide with this monthly event. Normally I would be put to bed at 7pm while my parents went out and the hotel owner kept an eye on me for them. The fireworks started at 8pm and lasted for over an hour and they were the best I have ever seen. By the time we got back to the hotel it was about 10pm and I felt really grown up being allowed to stay up until that time.

Also I used to look forward to our usual trip to Bude, Clovelly and Westward Ho on the Grey Cars coach. The roads were so narrow that the coach touched both sides of the hedgerows in places and I thought it was so exciting. Frequent stops had to be made, especially when negotiating the narrow lanes over Dartmoor. Oncoming traffic could not pass the coach and had to reverse until a pull in could be found to allow the coach to pass. This happened repeatedly but it was great fun watching the manoeuvres when some drivers hadn't a clue how to reverse. When we came up against another coach or a lorry the drivers would get out and have long debates on who had the shortest distance to reverse to a pull-in and these could sometimes get rather heated. But it was a splendid view sitting in the coach as we could see far away over the hedgerows.

Bude had a lovely sandy bay but as that was our lunch stop we didn't have much time on the beach. It was also quite a challenge at Clovelly to get down the cobbled street to the sea in the time the coach was allotted to stop there. But we always took up the challenge and we were tired out rushing back up the steep hill to catch the coach before it left for Westward Ho. The beach there was miles of golden sand and we usually managed to have a swim before getting fish and chips for our tea. Then back on the coach for the return trip across Dartmoor to Paignton. This was another special late night for me as the coach rarely arrived back until 10pm. That was always a super day out which I will always treasure and never forget. There was no chance for my father to mistreat me with so many other people around.

However all good things come to an end and it didn't seem long before we all piled back in the Austin 7 for the drag back home and that was always a big low for me. The summer holidays seemed to pass quickly for me and all too soon I was back at that dreadful school that I hated so much. I seemed to be taunted, ridiculed and bullied for most of my time there and it was a great relief to me when my father came home one evening when I was nine years old, to say that we would soon be moving back to Farnborough, where he had been offered more money at the RAE and with better prospects. The house at Cheltenham was privately rented, but the RAE had a lot of its own houses that it rented to its employees. So it wasn't long before we were all on the road again back to Farnborough. My only regret was moving away from Gran Cook who had been a tower of strength to me and helped me get over some of my darkest periods.

CHAPTER 5

Growing Uncertainty

From what I remember, the move and drive back to Farnborough in the Austin 7 went well and as it was all paid for by the Civil Service, my father even seemed quite happy for a while. I stayed with my Gran Cally for a few days while they got the house sorted out and was well into the cider and beer down in the cellar of her pub, The Prince of Wales in Aldershot. I was always happy down there and no one seemed to check on me so I helped myself without restraint!

The RAE house had three bedrooms and was bigger than the house in Cheltenham and it was also in much better condition as I couldn't see the sky through my bedroom ceiling as I could in the previous one. My bedroom was also bigger and I think it was warmer than the last house as well. It had quite a nice sized garden so I thought it would be all right for my playing and sunbathing.

These houses were built in strict military order in parallel blocks with eight houses in a block like the barracks that were the soldiers quarters. This stemmed from the fact that the houses were built by WW1 prisoners of war under the supervision of the army and so were called "Gerry Built". I never understood why this was a derogatory term because these houses were pretty good for their day. They were all in lines with a road between the front and back gardens of each line. The first line was built close to the RAE perimeter fence which had a gate for the use of the house employees. This was great because the travelling time to work and back was practically nil, unlike all the expensive and time consuming commuting that most of today's workers are forced into. These houses can still be seen and are occupied to this day but are now privately owned. They are still called Pinehurst Cottages but the MOD sold them off when the airfield changed hands in the late 1980s.

The really great news was that Gran Cally had also recently moved into Pinehurst cottages because as well as running the three pubs in Aldershot she was also employed by the RAE, so she qualified to rent one of their cottages. Along with other women, Gran used to paint dope onto the canvas of biplane wings to strengthen and preserve them. Her pub opening times were limited to two hours at lunch time and four hours at night so she juggled both jobs. I don't know how she did it, but it was great for me because I got to see a lot more of her now that we were living closer again. I would often call in to see her and she was always glad to see me too. At least this helped me when I was missing Gran Cook in Cheltenham so much.

The bad news was that it was in the same area as when we lived in Farnborough before. This meant that I had to go back to the same school that I had attended previously so I was back with all the teachers and children that I had had so much trouble with before. But I was very relieved when I spotted one welcome face in the playground, Alan, who was still at the same school. He was a year older than me and got me out of many bullying situations both inside and outside school. He was twice the size of me and others would think twice about taking him on.

Between classes at playtime I would try to keep a low profile or hide in the toilets or something. But I often got dragged off, stripped and tied to the school railings and punched, always in a part of the playground that wasn't overlooked by the Headmaster's office. Alan would often find me and help me get dressed and back to my class before the bell stopped ringing or else I would be up for the cane again. I think that was the bullies idea, to slow me up so that I couldn't beat the bell and would get punished again. He became quite friendly and he even came to play with me at home, and I used to go to play at his house as well. I thought he was a real friend and I could trust him.

Life at home was reasonable to start with, but after a while it steadily deteriorated to its previous state. My mother liked Farnborough better than Cheltenham and I think one reason was that she loved London and the bright lights and she used to be able to get there on the Aldershot and District coaches. They ran a regular service to Victoria coach station and the pick-up point was at the top of our road. However, my father liked Cheltenham better, as did I. Cheltenham had all the amenities of a big town and we only had to go two miles to find lovely countryside. Most of the countryside around Farnborough and Aldershot was owned by the MOD and it never seemed very inviting to me as it was mostly all scrub, sand and fir trees. My parents used to have endless arguments over where they preferred to live, always blaming the other for why they were unhappy wherever we were.

One thing Farnborough did have over Cheltenham was the Farnborough Airshow. The Farnborough Airshow was re-started after WW2 when I was eight years old. It was always the greatest event on the Farnborough calendar and lasted a whole week, usually in September. I remember my parents always took me to join the crowds of local residents who lined both sides of the Farnborough road just to see the upper class gentry sipping cocktails in their expensive chauffeur driven limousines. These would have different badges displayed on their windscreens depicting which of the many airfield car parks to which they were designated. Because of the sheer volume of traffic Farnborough would often come to a standstill and local entrepreneurs would take advantage of this and try and sell the captive visitors drinks, programmes and souvenirs. Local people would also open up their gardens as car parks to make some money by undercutting the official airfield parking prices.

Although the show was essentially for trade to sell our aircraft and components abroad, we the public could pay to enter the exhibition site during the weekend. Being an employee of the airfield, my father was always able to obtain free tickets so we often went on both days. The massive marquees housed models and components of the aircraft being sold and often had films of the aircraft in flight and how they were manufactured. Of course my father knew all about this and knew some of the representatives on the various trade stands who were only too pleased to demonstrate their wares. Also there were masses of free collectables on the stands and my father was usually able to get me a scale model of the plane concerned; these were often limited and very much sought after. Other free items would be balloons, caps, badges, stickers, brochures, playing cards, matches, pencils, pens, rubbers, mugs and many other things all with the aircraft manufacturers logos printed on them. I always walked home with a logoed carrier bag full of trinkets and memorabilia which kept me busy for weeks afterwards.

When it became too hot for us in the tents we would go outside and sit on a hill overlooking the runway to eat our sandwiches and watch the aircraft. Practice flying went on from first light and the displays were on for about 5 hours, so there was always plenty of flying to be seen. After my father had bought us drinks and ice creams we started to walk around the vast static display on the airfield. This comprised of both old and new aircraft, some of which we queued for to see their internal layouts and cockpits. There was also a large section devoted to the army showing all their latest vehicles and weaponry.

The air display for the public lasted anything up to five hours depending on the weather and consisted of all British manufactured aircraft. The aircraft manoeuvres were stunning to me at such a young age. The highlight for me being the British formation flying team. In 1947 I saw the first jet aerobatic formation team flying three de Havilland Vampires from RAF Odiham. Also very good in my estimation, came a three plane aerobatic team flying Gloster Meteors. In 1950 at Farnborough the Vampires performed an unbelievable display with their wing tips joined with rubber cords! They were watched by King George V1 and Queen Elizabeth along with 200,000 visitors. These jets brought a whole new era to formation flying and were a great success with the public. The first official Hawker Hunter aerobatic formation flying display team were called the Black Knights and gave a terrific show at Farnborough in 1955 with four planes using smoke trails. This team then merged with another Hunter display team and became the Black Arrows which eventually fielded sixteen planes. Not to be confused with the RAFs Red Arrows that we know today. I will never forget seeing the Black Arrows loop twenty-two Hunters in formation at Farnborough in 1958. We all went wild with excitement as this set a world record which remains unbroken to this day.

There were other aircraft that I loved to see at Farnborough Airshows and which became icons during my time at school in the early 1950s. The shining silver Bristol

Brabazon shook the whole of Farnborough when it took off and landed. It was the largest British aircraft ever built at this time and could only fly from Bristol and Farnborough where the runways were long enough. The Saunders-Roe Princess flying boat, which of course had no undercarriage, flew so low along the runway that I wondered how it stayed up. I felt so privileged to see this massive flying boat because only one was ever built and it only flew for a total of ninety eight hours before being taken out of service.

The Gloster Javelin was fast and loud and became our front line attack fighter for many years. It was supposed to be an all weather fighter and I thought it was so funny that it never flew at Farnborough if it rained. The Rolls-Royce Thrust Measuring Rig was nicknamed the 'Flying Bedstead' and it looked exactly that. It was a test-bed and comprised of a metal frame with a wheel at each corner and the pilot sat above two vertically mounted jet engines. It was very unstable but did just manage to hover. It was, of course, the forerunner of the Hawker Harrier. Lastly the de Havilland Comet was the first large passenger jet to enter service around the world and was far ahead of its competitors. It was very streamlined and later versions operated with the RAF as the Nimrod into the next century.

The army also gave a great display with their spotter and transport aircraft which dropped parachutists onto the airfield to engage in a mock battle with ground troops opposing them with their field guns and equipment. Unlike the RAF's Gloster Javelin, the army airforce flew whatever the weather and these mock battles often became the mainstay of the show, especially in bad weather when much of the flying display would be cancelled.

Considering that the Farnborough Airshow was the largest and longest running of its kind in the world, I thought the safety record was very good. I think I only witnessed two fatal crashes during my school years, though there have been more since. After these shows my father and I used to wend our weary way home through the dense crowds after a long day out. They were probably the happiest times I ever spent with him alone.

CHAPTER 6
Three Choices of Torture

At the age of 9 I still wasn't learning very well at school, and was still considered backward. I was having so much trouble concentrating when my head was full of what horrors would await me in the playground at the hand of the bullies, or what my father would think up to torture me with next at home and I was also often in a lot of pain from these events. There were also the beginnings of worries about the 11-plus exam so I had a lot of homework to do, and when my father was in he would stand over me while I did it. He got so exasperated and angry when I couldn't do it right that I became increasingly frightened of him because he would think up more and more painful ways to punish me.

He came up with the idea that he would give me three choices of how I was to be punished, all three involved me being stripped naked to start with. My first choice was to just have my hands tied behind my back, which didn't hurt much and did allow me to get to the toilet. But the bad news was that I would be left like that all night lying on top of my bed and whatever time of year it was I would freeze. I just couldn't manage the bedclothes with my hands tied tightly behind my back. The sheets were tucked in firmly and the blankets were too heavy for me to move.

My second choice was to have both arms twisted up behind my back, with my wrists tied together between my shoulder blades and both elbows tied tightly together. The rope round my wrists would then be pulled tight around my neck and the other end retied to my wrists, forcing my hands right up to the back of my neck. This did hurt a lot but my legs were still free and I could get to the toilet and I would have to stay on top of the bed in that position for 4 hours.

My third choice was the same as the second but the rope from my wrists was taken round my neck and I would be bent backwards like a banana and my father would pull both my ankles up behind my back and tie them together with the other end of the rope from my wrists. This was truly excruciating because he would pull it very tight and I could hardly breathe and the natural pull of my legs wanting to straighten would pull my wrists up higher around the back of my neck. Although this option was the most painful I would only have to endure it naked on the top of my bed for 2 hours. To add to the pain in this position, if I ever needed the toilet, my only option was to let go where I was. Then when my father returned he would shout at me and hit me for being so dirty and then untie me and straight away, tie me up in a different position for another hour or two. Also on the many occasions that I had colds or chest infections, the coughing and sneezing would greatly increase the pain. Of course I was totally unable to blow my nose so that increased my struggle to breathe and I often felt that I was suffocating and would have been better off to be able to die than endure it for any longer.

It was very difficult to get moving again when I was released from any of these positions and it was hard for me to make the choice when asked. One big consideration was that if I wanted to go out, especially if it was the weekend, even if it hurt me more I would often go for the third option. Then it wasn't for so long and hopefully I could do things afterwards, once I could get moving again. At the time, although I was frightened, I didn't really question what was happening to me. Nobody talked about such things then, so I just thought that this was every child's lot and that it was just the usual initiation ceremony that all boys went through to become a man. At least, that is what my father used to tell me over and over again.

I still wasn't enjoying my piano playing and I would sometimes get this choice of punishment just because he thought I wasn't making enough musical progress. He wasn't going to have me wasting his hard earned money on lessons.

School life was much the same as it was before and I was with a lot of the same boys and girls I already had reasons to be scared of. I still hated PT (physical training) as it was called in those days. I was never very strong physically anyway, but with repeated torture at school and home I was usually suffering from extremely painful injuries that rendered me completely weak and useless. So what chance did I have to climb the wall bars or ropes? I was constantly ridiculed and often caned for not trying hard enough. I hated PT so much that I would often skip the lesson and get the cane for that, but even that was better than all the ridicule at the hands of one particular PT teacher.

He was an ex-army paratrooper and I think he treated us much like he would have done if we were adult recruits. We were all made to do cross country running for miles because the headmaster was very keen on sport and his school always had to do well on the Aldershot and District sports days. I was hopeless at running, and this teacher would run with us and no matter how I tried, I always seemed to be at the back fighting for my breath and trying to keep up. He would shout and bawl at me to try harder and as I never wore vests, I was only clad in little shorts, shoes and socks and he would keep slapping me on my bare back which, of course, really hurt. Being ex-army he was a big muscular man and he used to make me fall over into the mud which he really seemed to enjoy, and being plastered in mud I would freeze in the winter. As if this wasn't enough, he would stand over me while I washed myself off in freezing water back at school and was then marched off to the headmasters office for the cane, again for not trying hard enough.

I hasten to add that I was not the only child subjected to this treatment. Many other children had no vests and we were still taken outside like this in sub-zero temperatures. We were then made to do things like jump over the tennis nets which were frozen solid and the ground was iced over. Several children ended up in hospital with broken bones but nothing was ever done to stop the teachers treating us like this. I got away with this because I refused to jump the net, realising that I couldn't clear it so I was naturally sent for the cane. But at least that was better than a broken arm or leg.

The last 4 or 5 children on the run usually came in for the cane, be they boys or girls. The headmaster would usually keep us outside his door, waiting in a cold corridor for about twenty minutes, still only in our shorts, though the girls and some boys did have vests. We were then ushered into his office by a couple of prefects, who always stayed with us. We were then lined up and the boys were told to drop their shorts, while the girls were allowed to keep their clothes on. Then we all had to hold our hands out and he walked down the line giving us three strokes on each hand. The girls would then be told to bend over and they would receive five more strokes on their behind. The boys, however, would be grabbed by the wrists by each prefect and hauled over the headmasters great mahogany table, face down in full view of the other children to receive their caning. I felt so humiliated and ashamed. What had I done wrong to deserve this treatment? My upper body was spread-eagled on the table with my arms being twisted and sat on by each prefect so I couldn't move. Even just this hurt enough. My bottom must have made a lovely target, hanging over the edge of the table with my legs dangling helplessly towards the floor. If I kept my legs still I usually received five strokes on my bottom. But if I moved my legs I would get caned on the back of them as well which were bare and cold.

I was then released by the prefects and I would just slide to the floor in a heap trying not to cry and completely unable to move. I couldn't believe that a few strokes of the cane could take so much out of me but he was strong and I just had no strength left. The prefects would then drag me out by my legs with my back rasping along the grit on the corridor floor and into the cloakroom. Here somehow I would manage to get my clothes back on. I think that is why I always felt so inferior and weak, because the other boys, and even the girls, were usually able to walk away but I was left a quivering wreck. It was probably because of these happenings that I was branded by the other children as spineless, weak and good for a laugh when they wanted to pick on somebody. To the teachers I think I was a dummy and a trouble maker who just wasn't trying. I just felt utterly dejected and lost and that I couldn't trust anyone at the school except for Alan.

I tried to tell my parents about the bullying at school and what I thought were the unnecessary canings by the headmaster and the degrading way they were carried out. My mother seemed quite sympathetic and said she would have a word with the headmaster. But my father said I was a good for nothing dummy and if that was the only way to get me to learn, then so be it. So I never mentioned it again and my mother never asked.

I longed for the school holidays, but even then I had to be careful where I went. The only time I felt really safe was when we went to the coast on a Saturday, as we often did. My mother drove the car and we both loved the sea. We usually went to Bognor Regis, Lee-on-Solent or Littlehampton because they were only about a 45 mile drive from Farnborough. This took about two hours in the little Austin 7. Getting over Bury Hill was the worst part in those days as it is very steep and long. In the summer we used to have to stop at the top to let the engine cool down and then refill it with water. I felt so free when we finally arrived. We had picnics, my father and I went for long walks, my mother and I sunbathed and I had no fears of being jumped on and hurt. There were too many people about for my father to hurt me while we were there. We all swam in the sea in the summer but we also went quite a lot in the winter too. I still swam until late into November as a rule, determined to prove to my father and myself that I was a man.

I still remember those swims vividly as I was quite scared sometimes when it was raining with rough seas and the wind cut through me as soon as I removed my clothes. On the other hand I felt great as I had the whole beach to myself, with no other people in sight. I took a folding chair from the car where my parents had parked on the sea front behind the beach huts to sit on while I changed into my trunks. I put my clothes under the chair to keep them dry and quickly made for the sea. By the time I hit the water it never felt as cold as I expected it to, maybe because I was frozen anyway! I usually managed about ten minutes of continual swimming, in quite rough seas sometimes, and I was exhausted by the time I got out and redressed in double quick time. I would freeze in the car afterwards with my teeth chattering for ages. But I felt strong in myself, having conquered my fears and thinking that not many people could have done what I had just done. If it was winter, we would go into a cafe and have fish and chips sitting down inside where at least I was able to warm up properly. I had trouble with this as we never ate out much and I always felt that everyone else was looking at me. I used to break out into a sweat and my mouth became so dry that I couldn't eat. I was so scared of not finishing it because I thought my father would punish me, but luckily he didn't seem to mind. He said it was all the more for him and took it from me quite happily! We didn't get home until it was bed time and I felt really strong and healthy after being in the salt water and sun all day. Even though I had brought back the same puny body as I had left with!

As an aside to the above, many years later when my father and I were looking around an oil painting exhibition in Bognor Regis, we saw a view from the very same place that I always swam from on the beach which was right at the end of a row of beach huts. The skies were dark and the sea looked ugly with the weather obviously blowing up for a storm. However we both liked the picture and it reminded me of the sometimes bad weather that I swam in. I bought the oil painting and it is hanging up in my flat to this day as a constant reminder of the lengths I used to go when I was young to try and become a man.

We still had our yearly trip to Paignton for two weeks in August and it seemed that we had much more sun then because I spent a lot of my time in the park sunbathing. It wasn't as crowded then either and although there was only a small car park behind the beach huts, there was always plenty of room for the few cars using it. We used to meet up with the same family every year and had beach huts next door to each other. They had a son, who was called John, who was the same age as me and he treated me very well. We used to go off on our own, walking over the rocks and cliffs with no shoes on and wearing just our swimming trunks. I used to love that. John was very kind and unlike most other children I knew, I don't think he ever made me feel bad by remarking on my puny body. He was well built and we used to have the odd trial of strength, which he always won of course. But he never made fun of me for being weak and always helped me if I needed it. Without his help I would never have been able to do some of the rock climbs that we did. I was very scared at times but he encouraged me and I felt so proud after I had done it.

We would sometimes go on excursions with John's family while we were there and a favourite one was the cream tea boat trip on the River Dart. We would gather together at Paignton bus station and catch a bus to Torquay harbour from where the pleasure boat started our day trip at 10am. This boat was a converted WW2 MTB (motor torpedo boat) with wooden seats replacing weaponry on the fore and aft decks. The wheel house was central through which one could enter the below-decks cabin. This had comfortable, soft, lounge type furnishings as it was out of the weather and had a bar with a food menu. These boats were fast as they were powered by gas turbine engines. One sensed their power when they were started up at the quayside, vibrating the whole boat with the engines just idling. On casting off and after slowly making our way across Torbay harbour, the throttles were increased and the vibration diminished. Having cleared Berry Head we turned to starboard (right) and headed for the open sea that had to be crossed before land was sighted again. Depending on weather conditions this could be a rough ride as the MTB was fast even through the rough seas. John and I found it exhilarating sitting on the foredeck seats near the bow with the wind in our faces and the spray from the waves often enveloping us. I doubt if that would be allowed these days with ever increasing health and safety regulations. But it was such fun back then!

When we had had our fill of wind and water we returned to where our parents were sitting in the dry on the aft deck. Here we had our packed lunches and sometimes went to the cabin below deck for snacks and drinks. It wasn't long after that before the coastline came into view and the throttles were eased off for our entry into the Dart estuary. The transition from the usually rough sea around the headland to the more or less flat calm of the River Dart often tempted more people to leave the cosiness of the cabin   for   a   seat   on   deck.

After gliding up the Dart for a while we would berth at a landing stage where anyone who wanted to could go ashore and stretch their legs for ninety minutes before the boat was due to leave. John and I would be given some money by our parents and allowed to go off on our own whilst our parents remained together. It was a good job John had a watch to keep an eye on the time. I couldn't and still can't bear straps around my wrist as I associated them with the ropes used to torture me. John did ask me why I didn't wear a watch but as I couldn't tell him the real reason, I just said I didn't want one.

It felt so exciting for me exploring along the river bank with John who I knew I could trust and I felt so free. On our return we passed through some shops where we bought a bag of chips each and before reaching the boat we had our favourite Mr Whippy ice cream to wash the chips down. We normally boarded with about five minutes to spare, and I could often see our parents starting to look anxious. However we were never late, the crew would slip the lines and we cleared the landing stage for our return trip.

Soon after leaving, the crew served us with our Devon cream tea with plenty of strawberries and lashings of cream. We all enjoyed this sitting on the foredeck in the calm waters of the River Dart. This worked really well as everyone had finished eating before reaching the rougher waters of the open sea.

As the throttles were opened up again the boat quickly gained speed and began to bounce and roll in the open sea. This motion suddenly made the upper deck less attractive to many trippers and they quickly headed for a more comfortable seat in the cabin. We could hear that the cabin bar must have been doing a roaring trade as the singing and laughing became louder and louder on our way back to Torquay!

I thought how a lovely pint of cider like Gran Cally's would go down well for me at this point to round the day off. Alas this was not to be as both our families stayed on deck all the way back. But it was worth it to see all the illuminations stretching from Brixham, through Paignton, to Torquay lighting up the whole of Torbay.

On berthing at the quayside at Torquay many of the trippers were still singing very loudly and had difficulty negotiating the gang plank onto dry land. Some of them fell into the first pub they passed and goodness only knows how they ever reached their hotels! Oh well, our families were sober and we boarded the first bus back to Paignton. Here we said our goodbyes to John and his parents until we met at our beach huts next day. Paignton was a picture all lit up with illuminations along the front, with floodlit cliffs and gardens at both ends of the beach. Walking back to the hotel I thought I could really get used to this and I went happily straight to bed when I got back to my room thinking that was the end of a perfect day.

I was sad when we had to leave Paignton because I always had a happy time there and I wished I had a friend like John at home. There was something special about him and even my parents liked him. They seemed to be happier and more relaxed when we were away and didn't keep on at me all the time. However it didn't last and when we got home my life changed dramatically back again with my parents reverting to their old ways and my father thinking up more ways to torture me.

CHAPTER 7

<u>Bound in Belfast</u>

Unfortunately for me the next year at school was time for the dreaded eleven plus exam which was in two parts. If you didn't pass the first part you didn't get to take the second part. But if you passed the second part it gave you entry into a grammar school which I understood was supposed to give you a better education than other schools. I knew my father wouldn't want me to fail and he had prepared more and more homework for me. I knew I hadn't got a hope of passing and I was terrified of what the outcome was going to be.

My results weren't improving in the classroom or in the homework. I think I was so aware of the pressure that I just couldn't learn properly and I wasn't the only child in the class in this position. I knew many more who were being pushed beyond their ability by parents and teachers and I used to feel sorry for them too. I don't know whether it was a coincidence or medically related, but many children in my class got very bad asthma during this period and were off school for long periods unable to breathe properly. I was very fortunate and didn't suffer from it but I couldn't understand why we still had to do PT outside in the autumn when so many children were obviously ill. I did pluck up the courage to ask the very foreboding paratrooper teacher one day why we had to do it; he said it was to make sure that not everyone turned out to be such a weak, spineless individual like me. And for once I didn't get the cane for speaking out!

We continued to go to the army swimming pool in Aldershot which I enjoyed. My mother had taught me to swim quite well, although I was still slow compared to most other children. It was not long before my fellow pupils really showed me how cruel they could be. I left school one night and it was getting dark as it was during the winter. We had all been swimming so of course we all had our towels with us. I got part way home when I was jumped on and frog marched by about eight girls and boys from my class, deep into some isolated woods.

A rope was passed around my neck, I was stripped naked and my wrists were tied behind my back. I was very cold and the autumn leaves were a carpet on the ground and they felt so cold with my shoes and socks removed. They forced me to the ground, held my head back and pinched my nose while they weed in my mouth and all over my face rending me blind with the acid spray in my eyes. With my hands tied I couldn't even try to wipe it out of my eyes. I was then backed up to a tree and the rope around my neck was tied to a tree trunk leaving some slack. They then produced their towels from their satchels and flicked them at my body, penis and testicles. I couldn't move much because the rope wrenched my neck. Being cold it was very painful and the gang had quite a time taunting me with me being a dancing bear and utterly weak. Eventually when they saw I could hardly stand, they released me and I just slid down the tree onto the leaves as all my strength had ebbed away. They threw my clothes at me and ran off laughing and joking. I eventually dragged myself out of the mire, dressed and staggered home. What a mess I was in.

My mother couldn't believe the state I was in and told me to undress for a bath. I tried to have a wee but my penis was so black and swollen I knew it would need attention. My mother was horrified, not only about the wields on my body but also that I was covered in creepy crawlies from the woods. I had a bath and I told her what happened on the way to hospital and she said she would see the headmaster. At hospital the police were called and I was pulled about and photographed. I was kept in hospital and had a catheter inserted into my penis finally enabling me to wee, to my immense relief.

I stayed in a few days until the bruising had started going down and the tube was removed. I was interviewed by the police again but I didn't say much because I was afraid of what the gang may do to me later if I told on them. My mother didn't get far with the headmaster either because I wouldn't name names. So it was left, no action was taken, they had got away with it yet again. I could never understand how any human being could derive pleasure from hurting and humiliating another in that way. But the good news was that I was off school for a month and when I went back, the outside toilets had frozen up so we were all sent home. Something to be said for the winter I suppose! The bullying at school died out for a period after that and I enjoyed a time of comparative freedom and went round to my friend Alan's house for tea and he came to my house sometimes too.

However, the first part of the dreaded eleven plus exam was due and I duly sat it. I was completely lost on most of it and I could easily have left the classroom after half an hour as I had done all I could of the paper, which wasn't much! My father immediately wanted to know how I got on when he came home and I thought I'd better say I wasn't sure in case he threw a tantrum. He wasn't very pleased because I knew he had his mind set on me going to grammar school. I was so nervous I was shaking in the exam and even if I had known all the answers, I doubt if I would have been able to write them down properly.

Just after this, in the school holidays, my father took me to Belfast where he went on business to the Shorts Aircraft Factory on behalf of the RAE. I wasn't asked if I wanted to go, I was just told, so that with me being out of the way meant that my mother could indulge more easily in her shopping trips to London. I hoped that being away from home may mean that my father was in a better mood than usual. But that proved to be a very false hope indeed.

It was frightening when we alighted from the ferry to be confronted by armed police and we were stopped many times between the docks and our hotel for identity checks. That made me feel very nervous for starters. We stayed one night and a hotel employee looked after me while my father was at work during the day. She used to take me to the shops and the park, but even though she was kind, I never felt at ease with so much security around. I was used to soldiers at home around Aldershot but I never felt as threatened by them as I did in Belfast. This was different.

The hotel was very plush and it was the first time I had seen so many knives and forks on the table for so many courses each served by high speed waiters. I couldn't eat half of it but my father ate what I didn't, so he was happy. We then retired to the bedroom and he put the wireless on loud. He told me to undress as if I was going to bed. Then he told me that what he was going to do was a necessary part of my growing up into a strong man and that as my father it was his duty to make a man of me.

To my horror he produced two ropes from his suitcase and tied me in many different positions pulling the ropes tighter and tighter. He said the longer I could endure without crying or screaming the better man I would become. Now I knew why the wireless was on so loud. I did try to stay quiet but I remember pleading with him for mercy and crying uncontrollably. I felt so trapped and afraid. I had nowhere to hide and I was so vulnerable without my clothes. After about half an hour of this treatment, by which time I was much weakened, he ordered me to sit on the bed. He then tied my wrists together in front of me and told me to lie on my side. He pushed my head to my chest and drew my wrists up behind my head which hurt a lot. My ankles were already tied together and he drew them up behind my back and tied them to the rope securing my wrists. I was bent backwards like a banana and the pain was awful in my shoulders, neck and back. He said he was pleased with me for not crying and if I could endure for one hour it would make a man of me. But this was a lie. He started tickling me all over and he tightened the ropes because my wriggling had slackened them. I screamed out and he gagged me with a cloth so that I could hardly breathe.

After an hour he released me and told me to make no sound. But I was on fire all over and too weak to move. Even after all that he said that I would never be a man and told me to wash and get to bed as we had an early breakfast booked. I rolled off the bed, crashed onto the floor and he just lashed my back with a belt to get me moving, which I did, saying I was spineless. I couldn't wash properly but I managed to get into bed totally exhausted and in excruciating pain. I was woken by him flinging the bed clothes off me, gripping my left bicep hard, dragging me out of bed and telling me to get dressed as we were late for breakfast. This was a man who wanted to train to be a church minister. He had no compassion in his heart at all.

We had a big breakfast, packed and walked through the crowds, police and soldiers to the docks and boarded the ferry and I was very relieved to leave. The crossing to Liverpool was rough and many people were ill, but my father and I were thankfully all right. I had a nice train ride back zipping through the countryside and my father told me not to tell anyone how he was trying to make a man of me. He needn't have worried as I was far too scared and humiliated to tell anyone.

We had a taxi home from the station at Farnborough and my mother asked me how I got on. I said all right - mostly, and she knew what I meant when she saw me get ready for bed. I was bruised on my biceps and I could barely move. I had wields across my back and for once she actually held me in her arms as if she was really concerned. But she didn't ask me what happened. As always, nothing was said to my father either. It was many years later that I found out that this was not a normal family occurrence and I wondered why did my mother never step in and stop this happening to me? Maybe she was scared of him too? But unfortunately for me it happened many times more when I was taken to Northern Ireland by my father. Each time getting worse in the torture.

Our trips to the south coast were a welcome change from life at home and school and I managed to get into the sea even if it was raining. We went to Paignton this summer, but I still had to go to bed early despite getting older, except for firework night, so that I was out of my parents way. It was so good to get away from all the chores at home, the homework, the housework, the gardening and the dreaded music practice. There was a lot of mail when we got home which was put aside until they had unpacked and we'd had some food. I was playing outside when I heard this awful commotion with them shouting at each other. I listened outside and this time my mother was pleading with him not to hurt me and saying it wasn't my fault that I hadn't got the brains that he had. He was ranting on that I was a good for nothing, dumb kid that would end up as a dustman if he didn't beat some sense into me first.

It then clicked that my eleven plus exam results had been in the pile of mail, so I ran round to my uncle's house who didn't live far away. I got on well with Uncle Ol and often wished he was my father instead of his brother. But he said my father would be even more angry if he didn't take me back. Ol had been a tank gunner in Africa during WW2 and spoke to Rommel many times after being taken prisoner. Rommel used to tour the prisoners compounds to make sure that they were being treated alright. Later when Montgomery started pushing Rommel back, the prisoners were taken with them and Ol ended up in Poland in atrocious conditions which changed him forever. But despite this, when he returned he married but sadly they never had children. He was a compositor by trade, a type setter for the printing presses at Gale and Polden in Aldershot, a high class printer. They were a leader in their field with the first to use colour printing presses. But Robert Maxwell bought them up and closed them down in the 60s as he didn't want their competition. This was a highly skilled job and required a seven year apprenticeship and the family was very proud of him. He was a keen supporter of Aldershot football club and took me to see a lot of their league matches. We also used to meet at my grandmothers to do her garden and sometimes at Christmas, which was often fraught with danger. But back to my eleven plus results.

Ol came home with me and tried to put in a good word for me but my father told him not to meddle in his affairs and showed him the door. I got a good grilling for not passing the first part of the exam and was banished to my bedroom. He later came back with some neck ties, rope, a belt and a foul temper. He opened my free standing wardrobe doors and tied a rope to my ankles and a tie to my wrists. I was then told to stand spread-eagled facing the doors while he tied my wrists to the top wardrobe door hinges and my ankles to the lower hinges. The leather strap soon hit my naked body from shoulders to calves while he vented his full fury on me. When my legs gave way, he left me hanging by my wrists. It was all over in a few minutes and about half an hour later he released my wrists and I crashed awkwardly to the floor as my ankles where still tied.

He left me like this for another half hour and then came back and pushed both my hands up behind my shoulder blades and tied both elbows together. I was in indescribable pain. He then untied my ankles and told me to stand up but I was so weak it took me ages and he sarcastically applauded when I finally managed to stand up. My mother then came in and a big argument ensued and they both went downstairs ranting and leaving me in a heap on the floor with my elbows still tied. My shoulders were on fire and I was very cold and much later my mother released me and, after washing my cuts, she told me to go to bed. I was just glad it was all over as I was utterly exhausted.

Later in the night I woke up looking into my mother's face. Apparently I had been having a nightmare and was thrashing about until I was dripping with sweat. These nightmares still haunted me until well into my 70s. For many, many years I dreaded going to bed as every night the horrors of my childhood came flooding back to torment me in my sleep. I had an overriding fear that I could never be a man. That hugely affected how I felt other people saw me and hindered my relationships with anyone. The nightmares also limited what I could do and where I could go, so holidays even as an adult, rarely happened.

I'm afraid my father never forgave me for failing the exam and our relationship deteriorated even further, if you can believe that was possible. He looked into paying for me to go to the grammar school but was advised that I wasn't up to it for which I was thankful. I dreaded to think what he would do to me if he was paying and I was still no good. I think most of his friends' children passed and he felt he couldn't hold his head up to them. I just couldn't live up to his expectations.

A while after this, I had an accident at school. I was helping to push up one of those long swinging planks on which a number of children could sit, when a big boy started pushing at the other end. I was gripping the bar tightly and went up with it and then it came crashing down onto my left knee on the rough gravely surface. I looked down and there was a great chunk out of my knee above the kneecap, which I could see sticking out. Somebody went for a teacher and she put a great wadge of cotton wool on it and a tight bandage. It was very painful and the headmaster took me to Farnborough hospital lying in the back of his big Ford Pilot. The headmaster went in and returned with two nurses carrying a stretcher and I was bleeding a lot by now. In the hospital the doctor cleaned it up, got the grit out and pulled the wound together with stitches and U hooks that hurt a lot, while the nurses tried to hold me still. It was so painful and I was so frightened at being held down by the nurses as well.

The headmaster took me home in his car and told my mother the story and later my father was furious with me for acting about in the playground! I was supposed to keep my leg straight and up if possible. But my parents wanted to go to the coast every weekend and insisted that I went too even though at 11 I was well old enough to have stayed at home on my own. I remember bouncing all the way to the coast and back in the Austin 7 with my leg straight along the back seat, it was agony. Though I was fortunate when my father sold the Austin for more than he had bought it for new in 1932 and bought a new Standard Eight, in black with red interior. I was so pleased because it had better springs than the Austin and got us to the coast quicker too. It also had a boot which meant that I didn't have to have the luggage packed all around me when we went on holiday. I could actually move around a bit too! It was a good car except it was poor at starting, especially in the winter, and over the years we spent many hours pushing it when the battery was flat. It had no heater, but I think anti-freeze came in about then, so we didn't have to drain the radiator out so often when the temperature dropped below freezing.

After a few weeks of visits to the hospital, it was decided that my knee was infected, so I had to have it opened up and cleaned out again which hurt as much as when I first did it! It was a very slow painful process getting it healed, with many more hospital visits to change the dressings. I was off school for five months in all so I had no schooling in that time except for my father's dreaded homework sessions. But thankfully, as I hadn't gone to grammar school, there were no further exams at school for me that year.

Soon after that I was knocked off my bicycle when I was cycling home by a wire stretched across a lane by one of the gangs. I went straight over the handlebars and heard my shoulder crack and the pain was intense. The gang stripped me while I was still dazed and two boys held me while a girl roughly handled my penis and testicles, tormenting me that I was no good because I couldn't perform. But I had no idea what she meant. My wrists were tied behind me and I was kicked in the groin and thrown in some stinging nettles and they left me naked with my shoulder in intense pain. I staggered home after dark and my mother untied me and took me to hospital. I was x-rayed and also pulled around, photographed and interviewed by the police, but I didn't say much as I was too afraid of reprisals. The police had no compassion and had no concern how much they were hurting or embarrassing me. My shoulder was broken and my so called private parts were a mess. I never felt right in that area again until much later in my life when my problems were finally diagnosed and I had an operation to try and put things right. I was off school for a few weeks and when I returned my arm was still in a sling. I couldn't do PT but that was great and the bullying by that particular gang thankfully stopped after that.

A while later, my father was offered more money to return to work at Gloster Aircraft near Cheltenham. It also pleased him to be away from his friends whose children had passed the exam. I was happy that I would see my Gran again but to my horror the rest of my life got worse. My father was going to send me to a boarding school even though my mother said I wasn't the right type for one. He found one and received confirmation of my place just before we moved back in the autumn of 1952. I was 12 years old. I was glad to go back to Cheltenham because in Farnborough I was frequently being stripped by gangs of girls and boys at school and on the way home. I was often tied to railings or trees, beaten, punched and sexually abused. So the thought of getting away from them was a relief, though I would miss my times at the pub with Gran Cally. I spent a lot of time at the pub while my parents were preparing for the move. I used to drown my sorrows with cider which helped to dull the pain. Amidst all this I did manage to pass another piano exam, I forget which one, and this actually pleased my parents for once. This didn't result in praise or reward of any kind, just less punishment for a while.

Just before moving, we had our annual trip to Paignton and we met up with my friend John and his family. It was a lovely summer, but not surprisingly after all the torture I had been put through and breaking my shoulder I was still having trouble with my arms and shoulders. John helped me to do the gentle exercises that he showed me and stayed with me while I swam. I remember lying in the hot sun on my front in the park while John gently massaged my shoulders. It was the first time I had experienced anything innocently kind like this from another child. After a fortnight of this treatment I went home feeling good and I actually felt quite strong for a change. My father for once had been no trouble to me over the holiday. Probably because I had managed to pass my music exam and he was always much more relaxed at Paignton. Unfortunately back in Farnborough I fell off my bicycle and banged my front teeth on the pavement which led to me developing an abscess and I had to have several of my top front teeth taken out. The denture had been made beforehand and it was put straight in after the extractions which was very painful. However my own teeth had stuck out and the denture actually looked much better. Of course I got taunted by the other children for having dentures at my age and they all demanded to see them.

It was not long after we got back that my father took me to the Farnborough Airshow again. There were many new planes out every year. Unlike now, there were many companies who made the whole aircraft themselves. One of these was de Havilland and they had one of their new planes called the DH 110 flying in the display. This was a twin boomed plane with a single jet engine in the fuselage and their chief test pilot, John Derry, flew it and his wife was there to see it. It was one of the fastest planes of its day and it took off with a great roar from its jet engine and flames coming out of the exhaust.

But suddenly during a tight turn over the airfield, the plane disintegrated with bits flying in all directions. We had been watching from a hilltop in front of a display tent and it was too late when we realised that the jet engine was heading straight for us. Many people ran from the top of the hill, down one side to the bottom. But the engine plunged straight into the foot of the hill, leaving a great crater where many people had sought refuge. My father had pushed me to the ground where we were, on top of the hill and he lay on top of me. This was the first and last time I ever remember him trying to protect me, but he would never speak about it afterwards. We both escaped any injury, even from the engine debris which flew a long way in all directions. When we got up I saw a frightening scene of utter carnage and devastation. People were dazed and crying and didn't know what they were doing. It was awful to see so many injured people suffering. There were so many people that the rescue services had difficulty in getting to the scene. My father did what he could for a man who was lying on the ground injured and when the rescuers relieved him, we made our way home. I think we were both in shock. We called in to the doctors on our walk home as we were in such a state and he gave us some pills. The 2 crew members were killed along with 29 on the ground and 60 spectators were injured. Safety regulations were tightened up after this and planes were stopped from flying towards the public whilst doing their display. We still went the next year as it was a big local tradition in Farnborough. We saw many more accidents over the years but none as bad as that one.

Not long after the airshow, we moved back to Cheltenham into a three bedroom rented house which was in quite good order. The old scullery and range had been replaced with a kitchen with a gas cooker and had open coal fires in all the rooms which was very up-market in those days. I went up to my bedroom and stood there in its emptiness and wondered what this chapter of my life would bring and felt a growing sense of dread.

CHAPTER 8

Adolescent Anxiety

This period of my life was one of growing anxiety and confusion for me. Why had I been put on this earth and where was my life supposed to be leading me. The fear of boarding school was uppermost on my mind and my self-esteem was nil.

I was very happy to be sent to Gran Cook's for a few days and nights while my parents sorted the house out. She made me so welcome and as always we had a great time together. We went to the shop to get the accumulator to get the radio working and she took me to the pictures and I was very happy to be with her again. I had never felt loved by my parents and didn't understand what it meant. I had always felt that I was a nuisance to them and wondered if my birth was planned at all. Maybe it wasn't. They didn't seem to want me around at all, that was for sure. Perhaps it was a convenient way out of my mother having to work during the war as the other women of her age were required to do. Then she could still do her hobbies and go on her shopping trips under the guise of looking after her child. I will never know. But I did know that my relationship with Gran Cook was great. She enjoyed my company and I enjoyed hers. This was real love and I was so sad when I had to leave and go back to the new house.

Life continued with compulsory music practice and as it was the summer holidays, I had not had the chance to meet anyone yet, so I had no-one to play with either. I was also afraid to go far because of the gangs I knew from before. But one lovely hot, sunny afternoon I couldn't resist venturing out to the nearby woods. Sadly they had been waiting for their chance and I was set upon by a mixed gang. I was only wearing a shirt, shorts, socks and shoes which were quickly removed and I was spread-eagled on the ground. They twisted my arms and legs and made me lie face down. The boys had roped two branches of a tree together to form a cross and this was laid on my back, my arms were tied to the crossbeam and my waist was tied to the stem. I was hauled to my feet bending double as the stem was too long and desperately tried to keep my feet as I knew that if I was pushed onto my back I would never be able to get up. After a while I was so weakened that they got me on my back anyway, calling me yellow and a coward. I tried to kick them, so they tied my ankles to the stem while they tickled and punched me and then left me. I was completely unable to move as I was bound hand and foot.

Thankfully they came back later but abused me again before untying me and still taunting me with their spiteful words. When they finally left I struggled to my feet and lay full length in a nearby stream to clean myself up and then stood naked in the sun to dry myself before struggling to get into my clothes. As usual they warned me not to tell anyone. Gran would have listened but I didn't want to bother her with all my troubles as she was so busy with all her work. I thought I'd endured quite well really, lasting out a long time until I finally gave in to their demands. What bothered me most was what the girls were saying when they were handling my testicles and penis, as if something was wrong with them and saying I would never be a man. These body parts were never spoken about at home or at school and I had never seen any other boy's body so had no comparison. These girls had posed another big question for me. I was already haunted by the fear of never becoming a man thanks to my father, but was I abnormal as well?

With these thoughts swimming round my head I duly arrived home and my mother told me to do my piano practice. I couldn't concentrate as my whole body hurt so much. She said it was awful. It was a blessing that my father wasn't in as I couldn't have taken any more punishment from him as well. I started to wonder whether I was sane. Was everyone else evil or was there really something wrong with me? And that worried me as well.

Meanwhile, we were settling into the new house and I was helping to get the garden in shape. I helped my father make cement paving slabs in wooden moulds and curb stones for the lawn edges and flower borders. We also had a greenhouse at this time and my mother loved flowers, so I used to help her plant seeds in wooden seed trays, no plastic then of course. It was nice and warm in the greenhouse. It wasn't heated, but it only needed a bit of sun and I was happy to be in there! The summer was busy in the garden and although I wasn't very strong, I used to like digging and preparing the ground for the marigolds and petunias that we had grown in the greenhouse. We also took many cuttings off our old geraniums and I was kept busy watering all these plants. I also helped my mother make our own cement flowerpots and tubs by bending thin plywood as formers. The pots were usually about 25mm thick and I couldn't lift the big ones so I had to roll them on their side to their allotted position before filling and planting them up.

All too soon it was time to report to my new boarding school. My parents took me and we all looked round the school with the headmaster. We were shown from the kitchens to the dormitories and I was frightened at the idea of having to sleep in the same room with lots of other boys. It was a big school with many corridors and I noticed the usual torture frames in the sports hall, folded back on the wall with ropes hanging from them ready for the dreaded PT lessons. It had large sports fields outside as well and the headmaster said that sport was high up on his priorities and expected his pupils to represent the school with pride. That was not what I needed to hear.

My mother drove us home in the little Austin 7, grinding up some of the hills in bottom gear and we pulled up at Gran Cook's house. The good news was that I was staying with her for a couple of days before starting at the new school so I got out very happily. Gran welcomed us and we all had a cup of tea and a cake before my parents left. I told Gran about the school and she could see that I was worried about it and tried to reassure me that I would be all right there. But I wasn't happy at all. I stayed 3 or 4 nights with Gran, the best nights for a long time. I slept well, cuddled up to her in her warm, comfy bed and we went to the pictures, had a picnic, went for walks and played card games. She showed me how to play Whist, Newmarket and Bridge. I was so happy and I used to curl up in the chair with Smutter the cat and she would always be there to welcome me home whenever I had been out. My mother was never there when I came home from school so this was really lovely. I was very sad when my parents came to take me back home.

I had a day or two at home and I was told to practice the piano for most of the time because Gran Cook didn't have one and my father didn't want me getting behind and out of practice. My father had also fixed up with the headmaster for me to receive my piano lessons at school to take me on to the next grade exam. The dreaded first day came and after my father had given me a lecture about behaving myself, he stayed behind and my mother drove me to the school. We drove up the long imposing driveway and as we stopped in front of the huge oak doors, I remember thinking that it looked like an old workhouse. We collected my baggage and were ushered into the headmasters office. We sat down and after a short chat with him, my mother left. I felt so small and alone. I was soon being shown to my bed and where the lockers were. The headmaster looked at what little luggage I had and asked me why I hadn't got a full school uniform yet. I said I didn't know, which was true but I suspected that my father wouldn't spend money on it if he could avoid it. Not that it bothered me. I didn't like being regimented and made to look like everyone else. I was an individual and was well used to not fitting in.

I was taken to my class room and introduced to my teacher and all the pupils. I was very shy and felt totally out of my depth. I can't remember a thing about the lesson and it was then time to sample the school dinners. It was some stewy mess like Lancashire Hotpot and the cabbage was like mud. For pudding it was figs and prunes and the prefects, who were also dinner monitors, said I had to eat it or I would have to answer to my dormitory prefect that night and be reported to the headmaster, which would certainly mean the cane. But I hated figs and prunes so I refused. Then I was duly marched along to the headmasters office, where I had to hold my hands out at arms length and soon found out how hard he caned. Not the best way to start my first day at school I thought! But it wasn't the first time I had had the cane on my first day.

I can't remember the rest of the day until it was bedtime, except that I ate all my tea. The prefect told us to get undressed for bed and all the dormitory taunted me because I hadn't got any pants, vest or pyjamas, so I stood there naked. Eventually they let me get into bed. Not long after, I was hauled out of my bed, both my hands were twisted up behind my shoulder blades and I was rammed up against a wall. My head was pulled back and they stuffed something into my mouth to gag me. I was then spread-eagled on the floor while they tickled me. Then I was thrown onto my front on the floor and had to arm wrestle them all and of course I was so weakened I didn't stand a chance. I was then dragged to my feet and flicked with towels while my arms were pulled tight across my back. I was thankful that they didn't aim for my private parts like the girls had done so many times before. The girl gangs had always been much more cruel than the boys. But here I was completely at the mercy of about 12 boys. I was then thrown onto the bed, un-gagged and told not to tell anyone. There was a lot more taunting about being a weakling before they finally put the lights out and I tried to get to sleep. But I was too terrified to sleep.

After a fitful night's sleep I was pulling my shorts on after getting up when the prefect said to take them off. I had to wash naked while others were clothed and splashing me with cold water and trying to keep me from the basins. Apparently the last one dressed had to do errands or other nasty tasks for the prefects all day. As I was last of course, the prefect threaded his arms through mine behind me, pushed my head forward with his hands, lifted me off the ground and others punched me in the stomach while I hung naked and helpless. I was then dumped and told to dress and make my bed. During breakfast I knew I couldn't last long here. Whilst in the PT lesson the teacher spotted all my wields from the towels and I was taken to the lady nurse in the sick bay. She wanted to know how I had got them but I wouldn't say because I had the feeling that I couldn't trust her. So she covered the sores with cream, pulled my shorts down and roughly creamed my private parts though I am not sure why that was necessary. She said to come back next day and though I had to, I was very wary of her as she was so rough.

At least the PT lesson was nearly over when I returned, so I didn't have to endure the wind that always seemed to be blowing a gale there for too long. I don't know whether anything was said but I was left alone for a while after that. But I didn't make any friends there because I never felt I could trust any of the boys or the prefects ever again. My music teacher was probably the best person I got on with as he was kind and encouraging. But if I learned anything else at this school, it was through fear.

All too soon I was in trouble yet again. One morning the boys had dragged me out of bed early and had made me 'come' whilst pinning me on my bed. It was all over my stomach and they rubbed my hand in it and spread it over my face just before the prefects came in. They dragged me down to the headmaster and he said I was a pervert and this warranted a public punishment as it was so serious.

He told me I would miss breakfast and after a bath from the nurse I would receive my punishment in public. I was dragged naked to the dreaded nurse who roughly bathed me in freezing cold water and I noticed my testicles had completely disappeared causing great discomfort. I was marched back, still wet, to the main hall where all the school had assembled in front of the climbing frame, which had been pulled out from the wall. I was then lifted up off the floor, spread-eagled and my wrists and ankles tied to the frame. The headmaster then stood on a box and whipped me with a leather strap from my shoulders to my calves. I think I must have passed out with the pain because when I was taken down the hall was empty. I was dragged off by the prefects to the nurse, scraping along the floor on my raw back to be washed and salted again causing further agony. I was in a bad way by the time I got to bed that night and had nightmares about it a lot.

Not long after this I developed a bad cold and chest infection and my mother was called to take me to my own doctor. We called in on the way home and after examining me, he said it was bordering on pneumonia and I would need bed and pills. He was horrified by the state of my body which still had cuts, wields and bruising from the thrashing. He asked me what had happened and when I told him, he said he would back my parents if they wished to make a complaint against the school. But needless to say, they didn't and it went no further. Maybe to them it didn't seem that extreme.

I was in bed for some time with pills to take and ointment to rub on my chest and all I wanted to do was just sleep. I was away from school for at least six weeks and although my father didn't give me any trouble over that period, he wasn't happy about me missing all that school time that he'd paid for. Although I was ill, I thought it almost worth it to miss school and when I did eventually return it was thankfully near the end of the spring term. Also I saw Gran Cook a lot more because she would call in when she wasn't working and we had some good times together as she always cheered me up so much. The rest of term passed with only minor bullying in the dormitory and I finished bottom of the class as usual. I got a lot of verbal abuse from my father when he saw the report at Easter but nothing physical. I think the words from the doctor may have frightened him a bit, though sadly not for long.

I was back again for summer term and after another caning session by the headmaster for being late dressing, I was once again dragged naked by the prefects to the nurse. I had been cut on my back and bottom by the cane and she washed me down roughly in freezing water and once again my testicles and penis got a lot of unnecessary attention. The prefects who were still watching then held my arms while she rubbed salt into my cuts which really stung. She put plasters on some of the worst cuts. When my ordeal was over I was given my clothes and marched back to my class where it was very painful to sit down. All this didn't do my education any good and I finished up at the bottom of the class again in my final term. After handing me my report the headmaster gave me his usual blasting about being thick and said that on second thoughts he'd take it back and post it as he couldn't trust me to give it to my parents. The next day I left with my mother in the car for six weeks of very welcome summer holidays. She asked me how school was and I said it was awful and that I'd been bullied a lot, but didn't go into details. She said she would talk with my father about it, but I didn't hold out any hope, especially when he saw the report. I expected him to take the usual reprisals against me, but for some reason nothing happened and I didn't understand why. Maybe for once my mother had spoken up in my defence.

I had now turned 13. It was good to be home again because my father went abroad with his work, so my mother and I spent quite a nice time together. I saw Gran Cook quite often and told her about the school and she said she would speak to my father about it. My mother also took me to London and we spent hours looking round the shops. Not my idea of fun, but it made a change!

About this time I was worried that when my penis got big my testicles tended to disappear and I plucked up courage to ask my mother if I was all right. She said it was part of growing up and that we didn't talk about dirty things like that. But I still worried that I wasn't normal. I was proved right when many years later I was diagnosed with undescended testicles which required an operation to correct. All I knew at the time was that whenever I was interfered with, or got really cold, they went up inside my body which was extremely painful. This of course just added to the multiple pains that were inflicted on me by my father and the various gangs when they interfered with me down there. I guess they just enjoyed the added pain that my own body put me through.

When my father came home from abroad we went on our usual summer holiday to Paignton and Gran came with us this time, which was great for me. Gran seemed to have a calming influence on my father and he seemed much more relaxed than usual and didn't take anything out on me when she was present. It was certainly a squeeze in the Austin 7 with Gran as well, but it was well worth it. It was so good to see my friend John again too. I told him about my boarding school troubles and he said it was a shame that he wasn't there because he would have stood up for me and I knew he would have. We had our usual great time of sunbathing and swimming in the sea. John and I spent many happy hours together walking the cliffs and over the rocks and beaches when the tide was out. We only had our swimming trunks on but I always felt so free and strong when I was with John.

One of our favourite walks was from our beach hut on Goodrington Sands, along the beach and up over the winding cliff walks and down to the harbour in Paignton. From the quayside we sat and watched the fishermen with their rods and lines who were only too happy to show us their skills. Having said that, we rarely saw them catch anything besides the odd clump of seaweed! The highlight was a lovely Mr Whippy ice cream which was always a race against time to devour before it melted in the hot sun of a July day. If we had any pennies left over we would have a play on the "one armed bandits" in the amusement arcade just off the quayside. Remarkably we nearly always finished up with a few pennies profit which we often invested in another ice cream between the two of us which was eaten on our way back.

Another popular walk for us was in the opposite direction along Goodrington beach and over the rocks at the base of the cliff to Broadsands beach. This could only be done at low tide and though we tried to dodge the waves, we were usually soaked by the time we got to Broadsands. However we always felt so strong and exhilarated after beating the elements and we soon dried out in the hot sun.

That was cause for another celebration where we bought another Mr Whippy ice cream each at the mobile shop on the sands. Broadsands is a lovely long, reddish gold sandy beach which was quite secluded and there never seemed to be many people there. John and I used to stretch out on the sand sunbathing and with my friend by my side, I felt so relaxed and unselfconscious. We had the odd trials of strength and arm wrestling, lying on our stomachs in the sand which John nearly always won. If I did win one, I knew it was only because he let me and did it to encourage me. With the tide coming in, we walked back over the cliffs, passing through a few caravan parks until we returned to our beach huts on Goodrington beach. These were great times for me and I will never forget them, or him. He was a real friend to me.

We had our usual coach trip by Grey Cars Coaches to Bude, Clovelly and Westward Ho which this year was a real scorcher on the bus all day. My parents usually managed to book one of the cooler days of the holiday for this trip but it didn't happen this time. The sun never went in which was great for swimming at Westward Ho but roasting in the coach as there was no air conditioning in those days. We were still all wringing wet when we got back to Paignton, even though it was around 10pm. Walking back to our hotel I heard my parents discussing going for a swim to cool off. I assumed I would be put to bed and they would go and I was shocked when they told me to get a towel as I was going swimming with them. The hotel was situated only about three buildings down the High Street off the main seafront road. Then we only had to walk across a green and the promenade before reaching the beach.

The illuminations were on so we undressed the other side of the beach huts on the main Paignton beach where it was all dark. I waited for someone to give me my costume but was taken aback when my parents headed for the sea stark naked! I hung back but I was beckoned by both parents to follow which I reluctantly did. Fortunately the tide was in and there wasn't much beach to cover before I was covered by the water. I found it surprisingly warm and my father said that was because the sea had come in over the sand which had been warmed by the hot sun all day. However I was very dubious of my father's intentions and kept a distance from him in the water. Fortunately all went well and we all had a refreshing swim and enjoyed ourselves bathing by moonlight on Paignton beach.

It was pitch dark and practically deserted when we ran up the beach to find our clothes. With only the noise of the gentle swell of the waves. I had the rare feeling of all being well in the world. It was still so warm that we never bothered getting dressed and walked the short distance back to our hotel bare foot, wrapped only in our towels. I will never forget the sensuous pleasure I enjoyed when the whole of my body was being washed with cool, clear sea water after a hot, sweaty, dusty day tour on the coach. I had the suspicion that it wasn't the first time my parents had done that as it seemed to come very naturally to them and I began to wonder why I was punished at home on so many occasions for being naked. I came to understand that this was a regular event after they had put me to bed while on holiday in Paignton.

Years later I found out that these nude bathing sessions were even more extraordinary as they were illegal! Beach huts were provided so that people could change their clothes unobserved by other beach users. People were not supposed to undress on the beach or sunbathe or swim naked. It all seems very prudish to me and people don't know what they are missing. I'm surprised at my father for breaking the rules like that but perhaps my mother, who was ahead of her time in so many ways, persuaded him.

Another thing we liked to do while we were there was to have rides on the top deck of the local buses to Babacombe and other nearer bays. It was great on the top deck as the views were stunning on the coast road and the bends were so sharp it felt as though the bus was going to turnover sometimes. Quite exciting when you are only 13! The weather was hot and sunny and the fireworks were as good as ever. John was such a good friend to me and I so enjoyed times that we spent together. He understood me, gave me confidence and never put me down. I was so sad when we had to leave but at least I had Gran to talk to in the back of the car which made things easier for me.

In the summers I would sometimes see one of my cousins, Bob, who was the same age as me but he thought I was a cissy because I wasn't as adventurous as he was. He used to want to climb trees and the steep hillsides near my home but I was too scared sometimes. He was the only one of the many cousins who lived in Cheltenham that I got on with and he never hurt me even though he was stronger than me.

That summer I decided to go to some disused quarry workings and practice some climbing on my own so that I could surprise Bob sometime. It was a lonely place and the sun was hot so I took my shirt off and laid on a wooden seat where I dozed off. Something woke me and I was staring up into the faces of the mixed gang of girls and boys that had bullied me before when I very first moved to Cheltenham when I was 7. When I saw them I really knew I was in for trouble. I was pinned to the seat while they removed my shoes, socks and shorts. I was made to stand up and bend over with one arm behind my back and the other in front of me. My wrists were then tied between my legs. I was in a crouched position with bent legs which I couldn't hold for long so I fell on my side. The pressure that my wrists had put on my penis had made it big and a girl tied a rope around it as well. Then they got me to my feet and the girl pulled me along with that rope. I was lead to a tree that was in the full sun. My wrists were untied and I was hauled up and my wrists tied again, this time to a horizontal tree branch with my arms spread wide apart. I was then left to hang with my feet off the ground, while the girl swung me to and fro with the rope on my penis until I 'came'. My body had learned long ago, that this was what was required and responded this way to fear and caused me great pain. After ejaculating my penis went small and the rope fell off. My ankles were tied together with a wet rope and the other end was tied to a stake, which had been driven into the ground by the boys with rocks. I then knew it was premeditated because where would they get a wet rope from? They must have seen me go up that way and made their plans, knowing from earlier times that I was an easy target and wouldn't tell on them. As the rope dried in the hot sun it shrank and I was stretched more and more and the pain was unbearable. My naked skin was also burning in the sun. I screamed out for mercy but they wouldn't release me. After what seemed like forever one of the boys took pity on me and untied the ropes round my arms causing me to fall in absolute agony onto the floor, completely unable to move. They all ran off laughing and left me there and I must have passed out.

The next thing I knew I felt something touching my ankles. I looked up and saw a dark skinned boy of about my age and he was well built, unlike me. He cut the rope from my ankles and gently helped me to dress. He then put his hands under my arm pits and lifted me up like I weighed nothing at all and rested me against the tree. Even in my pain I remember seeing the size of his biceps and envying him. How different my life would be if I had strength like his. He produced a big bottle of water and helped me to drink, all this time saying nothing. While he was so close to me I noticed how startlingly bright his eyes were. Though no words were spoken by either of us, I could feel overwhelming compassion radiating from his eyes. I had never felt anything quite like this before, even from Gran Cook. Then having tended to my immediate needs he was gone. Looking back I have often wondered if he could have been a dark skinned angel?

I passed out again and the next thing I knew I was being lifted onto a stretcher. How did they know I was there? Did the angel tell them? I will never know but they were horrified at the state of me. They kept asking me questions and doing tests and finally strapped me on the stretcher ready for the long walk down the steep hill to the road.

There were three medics, a woman and two men who carried me down the hill with difficulty. It was very slippery in places with loose quarry stone workings on the path giving a very loose foothold. After a bumpy ride we made it to the ambulance and I don't remember any more until I awoke in hospital with many people in uniforms looking down at me. I was being pulled about despite the pain I was in by the police so they could take pictures of me from all angles. I was also smothered with cream to alleviate my sunburn. Although everyone wanted to question me I must have been sedated, as I don't remember any more until the next morning.

The next morning after breakfast, I was taken for a bath by two female nurses and I was very scared. I tried to tell them I was frightened of girls; girls had always caused me so much more pain than the boys did. But they didn't understand so I just shook with fear. I couldn't believe the state of my penis and testicles, just a solid black mass of swelling and bruising yet again, which hurt a lot. Later in the day I had a catheter inserted to enable me to wee. The first visitors were my mother and my doctor who wanted to know what happened, as did the police. But I couldn't say anything for fear of more retaliation later, so I said nothing and they weren't at all sympathetic to me. I was so exhausted and in so much pain that I just wanted them all to go away and leave me alone. But that didn't seem possible and everyone else's requirements were put before mine. All those in uniforms, be they nurses, doctors or police were hostile to me. They were all cross with me as I wouldn't tell them the names of the kids who did this to me. I guess they were trying to do their job but I just couldn't say. I had no one who would defend me in the weeks and months ahead.

The muscles across my chest had been completely torn so both my arms were strapped across my chest. I couldn't do anything for myself so feeding and toileting were a nightmare. It was about 2 months before I could use my arms again. As the bruising went down, a couple of the nurses told me that they didn't want any wet beds, so they duly fondled me until I came. But to me it was no relief, just more all too familiar abuse and pain. My body duly obliged of course, as it had learned what was required at times like that to please the other people and get them to go away.

I left hospital soon after my arms were finally released and my mother drove me back to hospital a few times a week for massage and physiotherapy. Soon I was able to raise my hands as far as my eyes so I could at least feed myself. I did hear my doctor telling my mother that my shoulders and chest were badly damaged and I would probably never get normal use of them back again. This frightened me and I was determined to exercise to get some strength back despite the pain. The good news was that I missed a whole term at school and didn't go back until after Christmas. Much of this time was spent very happily with Gran Cook and Smutter, so that was great. I could still play the piano when I was at home and actually got a good result in my latest grade, which thankfully pleased my father. But when I was at home and trying to do my exercises, he took an unhealthy interest in watching me. I think he got a kick out of seeing me struggling in pain. Gran Cook tried to persuade my parents not to send me back to that boarding school, because she and I knew that I was going to be even more vulnerable than before. But they wouldn't listen to her and I had to go back, one more time.

Since leaving hospital I hadn't ejaculated again until I was forced to by the boys in my dormitory and the pain was horrendous. I also noticed and felt that my testicles never seemed to hang down at all anymore and were completely solid and always uncomfortable. I did manage to see the school doctor but he said that was normal at my age. I learned later, after many years of pain, that it wasn't normal at all. But at the time I had to believe him.

The prefects were getting me into trouble more and more and I was repeatedly caned for any reason that they chose to make up. I couldn't stand it anymore and one night I managed to hide my clothes in my bed and, when I thought everyone was asleep, I slipped out of the dormitory, dressed in the washroom, opened a window and stepped out onto the roof. I slipped down the tiles and managed a 10 foot drop to the ground. It was a heavy frost and I only had a shirt, a woolly, shorts and socks on but no shoes. However, I was determined to get to Gran Cook's house which was about 8 miles away and I started off across the fields and kept away from the road in case I was found to be missing at school. Luckily I came across a line full of washing in a garden under some trees and it wasn't completely frozen, just a bit damp. I donned two woollies, long trousers (the first I'd ever worn) and tied two towels around my feet which were absolutely freezing by then.

I was feeling quite pleased with myself as I set off again across the fields. It looked as though my third attempt to escape had worked without raising the alarm. My last previous two attempts had failed miserably when I was caught and mercilessly flogged in front of the whole school yet again. Fortunately I had a reasonable knowledge of the area and I stumbled on over the fields disturbing badgers, foxes and all kinds of wildlife lurking in the undergrowth. I disturbed a few dogs as well who started barking when I passed some of the farm houses. But thankfully everyone was tucked up in bed so nobody came out to investigate. I stayed near to the roads that I knew but kept inside the hedgerows in case I was pursued. I fell over many obstacles in the dark and my knees were soon cut and bleeding. I don't know how long the journey took me but it was certainly many hours of struggle and pain. However, the pain soon turned to sheer joy when I heard the unmistakable call of Smutter as he emerged from under a hedgerow. I had never been so pleased to see him. He must have sensed that I was coming as we were still well over a mile away from Gran Cook's house. He stayed in front of me and lead me his shortest way home. It wasn't always the best way for me though because he went through the hedges while I had to detour around them. But he always waited until I caught up again. The way he looked at me seemed to imply "What took you so long?". Eventually cold and exhausted (me not Smutter), we arrived at Gran Cook's and Smutter started making a loud noise.

Smutter kept up his rhetoric until the flicker of a gas light could be seen from inside and Gran opened the door. Later on she told me that if it hadn't been for his caterwauling she wouldn't have opened the door at that hour of the morning. So I had even more reason to be grateful to him. But he had told her on my behalf that she needed to come, and she did. As ever she took me in and was visibly shocked at the state of me. Gran re-stoked the range and gently bathed me and tended to my cut feet and knees while I told her of my great escape. We had a couple of cheese sandwiches together before we went to bed in her bed and she gently put her arms around me. I asked Gran not to let my parents send me back to that horrible school and she said that I would only go back over her dead body and she would speak to them tomorrow. That was what I needed to hear, because at last it looked as though someone was on my side and believed what I had said. She said `Don't worry you will be all right' and those words were the most reassuring that I had heard for a very long time. I fell asleep in her arms, utterly exhausted.

The next day, while I was slowly getting dressed, I heard Gran Cook downstairs talking to someone quite sternly I thought for her. I assumed that she must have a visitor. But when I got down I saw Smutter, already in his favourite chair in front of the range with Gran wagging her finger at him. Amidst all the confusion of the previous night Smutter had obviously slipped indoors out of the cold and managed to stay in without being spotted. Gran was not best pleased though he was soon forgiven especially considering his help to me in my time of need. After breakfast Gran and I walked round to my house. This was very slow as I hurt all over. Thankfully my father was out at work and my mother was very surprised to see us. We all sat down with cups of tea while Gran told the story and my mother agreed I shouldn't go back. She asked Gran Cook if she would have me for a few days while she discussed it with my father and the school.

I was so glad to hear that and we had a great time together as always and went to the pictures and I was so sorry when my mother came for me. When we arrived home my father was waiting at the table, he asked me to strip and I was terrified he was going to beat me again. He looked at the welds which were still very visible on my back and buttocks that I received from the last prefects' beating. He asked the reason for this and I said I had tried to run away before and this was my punishment. He said that the headmaster had told him that I was a spineless troublemaker, who needed to be kept in line with the strap sometimes. However my father told him that he was quite capable of keeping his own son in order and was paying for his son to be educated at school not thrashed as he could do that at home for nothing.

After a long lecture and still naked I was told that I would not be going back to that school and my heart leaped for joy. He said I wasn't worth the expense and had made arrangements for me to go to another school about a mile away. But that it would only be for a few months, as he had got another job in Farnborough and we would be moving back there again. I didn't know whether that was good news or bad, but I knew I would miss Gran Cook again. She seemed to be the only person who believed me, she had stood up to my parents on my behalf and had secured my release from that dreaded school.

I was frozen by the time my father told me to get dressed and not long after that I developed a chest infection and went to hospital again. After each thrashing at school I had been thrown into a cold bath before the salt was rubbed into my wounds. I was then made to dress while still wet and maybe that and the freezing escape had taken its toll on my body. I was in hospital for a month and then spent more time recovering at home or with Gran, so thankfully I never started at the school that my father had sorted out for me. I still went to hospital for massage and exercises and the female nurses couldn't understand why I was so frightened of them. I would only exercise with male nurses. My grandmothers were the only females I trusted.

When I had more or less recovered, I felt pretty fit except for my permanently weakened chest and shoulders. Sadly though, it was then time to say goodbye to Gran Cook and Cheltenham once again and return to Farnborough. I was once more in trepidation at what life would hold for me next, although I always held on to the hope that it may just turn out to be better than before.

CHAPTER 9

Teenage Insecurity

For some reason unknown to me we went to Newquay in Cornwall for our summer holiday that year instead of Paignton and I was very sad at missing my time with John as I know he would have built me up again after all my troubles. Instead I was mainly on my own most of the time. I really missed John's company during that holiday and I often wonder how life turned out for him as I had no more contact with him at all. The only consolation was that I did feel free to venture out on my own there and felt relatively safe. I found a secluded tree, which I practiced my exercises on, trying to strengthen my biceps. I swam as much as I could in the sea and I was doing well with the breaststroke, but I still couldn't get my arms over my head properly to do the front crawl. Although I didn't want to go, I'm sure I benefited physically and mentally for going. My father didn't give me any trouble either while we were away which was a big plus. We had a beach hut on Fistral beach which had two doors like a stable. We soon found out why when we spent half our mornings digging it out of the sand which had blown up against the lower door overnight. It was always windy with no shelter and when I was trying to sunbathe I found out what a spark plug must have felt like being sandblasted!

Of course the surfing was good with the sea being whipped up by the wind and my mother loved it. Maybe that's why we went there. But my father didn't go in the sea much and I thought surfing was a really cold game, wading out and hanging about for the right wave and then try and jump on the board. I noticed that people who stayed in for any length of time had wet suits. But though I loved the sea I was soon out trying to get warm out of the wind. We had coach trips around Cornwall and the hotel was nice, but I still had to go to bed early and there was no big firework nights to look forward to like at Paignton. When we returned home there was still quite a lot of summer holiday left and I had time to reflect on my growing uncertainty of why I was here and what my life was for. Was my life always going to be filled with fear and pain? I would have gone to bed quite happily if I knew I wouldn't ever wake up in the morning. But I didn't have too much time to think as I was given plenty of chores to do in the house and garden.

I spent a lot of the time with my grandmother in the pub and was able to concentrate on strengthening my arms and shoulders. It still took ages trying to wash my hair though as I couldn't keep my hands that high for long enough. Eventually, I broke through the pain barrier and was able to hang from tree branches in the garden with my feet off the ground for a second or two. Eventually I also managed one press up and I was so pleased. I still went for regular check-ups at the hospital for my knee and shoulders. They pulled me about quite a bit, but they were pleased with my progress and they said I'd done well in a short space of time. Rare praise indeed for me.

By the time I went back to school, I could do two press-ups and hang my body weight from a branch for four seconds, before the pain made me give in. I resumed swimming again with school in the army pool and my body gradually improved. I felt quite good because I had obviously benefited from a few months where I suffered no abuse, at home or school. This was the longest time without abuse that I had ever known.

Our new home was quite close to the RAE and was a rented, detached three-bedroom house, with a large garden and I was given the tiny box room for my bedroom. It had a vertical water pipe running behind the centre of my headboard and up into the ceiling. This was quite noisy every time water was running anywhere in the house. I was fourteen by now, and when I finally went to the local school I was one of only two boys in my class who were still in short trousers. For some reason my father wouldn't let me have long trousers until I was 15. I was taunted by girls and boys for my skinny legs, knobbly knees and sadly, the still obvious lack of pants.

It was good to be back near my Gran Cally once again, although I missed Gran Cook and Smutter very much. I was often at the pub at weekends and school holidays. Gran Cally always treated me well and even sometimes stood up to my father on my behalf. After that he would back off for a while, but never for long. I had the run of the large garden at the pub and the cellar with unlimited pints of cider on tap! We had several fruit trees at home which I used to exercise my arms and shoulders.

Then summer was over, but at least I wasn't back to the boarding school. The school took us to the army swimming pool in Aldershot and I realised how much I had missed that while we were in Cheltenham. It was good exercise for my damaged muscles and I really loved the hot showers afterwards. Being still so weak I was an easy target for the bullies. The most common torment was still having my arms twisted through the school railings. While I was held there in great pain some girls took it in turns to put their hands up my short trousers and squeeze my penis and testicles until I ejaculated, which resulted in a mess everywhere.

Every time I was made to ejaculate now it was very painful indeed and I tried my hardest not to even though it meant the torment going on for longer. I was sure this wasn't quite so painful before I was hung on that tree in Cheltenham and I was convinced that I must have been damaged inside. I was usually held captive until the bell at the end of playtime, so I didn't have time to clean up and had to sit in wet shorts with my penis still leaking. This was made worse because I had to sit next to one of the girls in class who regularly abused me and I was so scared of her because she was much stronger than me.

Needless to say, my learning was still suffering and there were 56 pupils in my class at this time so I didn't get much helpful attention at all. But at least this headmaster didn't give me the cane so often. One such time though was for persistent truancy. I left home for school on my bicycle and didn't arrive for three days out of five because I was so afraid of the girls catching me again. I just used to break down sometimes and couldn't take it anymore. If it was sunny I would go and find somewhere away from everyone, take my shirt off and sunbathe all day, feeling safe because I knew my enemies were in school. Then I would turn up at home at the right time in the afternoon. The headmaster wanted to know why I wasn't attending so I told him about the bullying. He said he would investigate but it still didn't condone truancy, so I got the cane anyway.

Without thinking I dropped my shorts and started taking my shirt off and he asked me what I was doing. I said that I had always been asked to strip for punishment or I would never become a man. He said that whatever others had said before was not for him to judge, but he didn't work like that. He asked me where my pants were and I said I didn't wear them and he looked quite shocked. He told me to put my clothes back on and while doing this I asked him how he was going to tie me up. When he said he wasn't going to tie me up at all I just couldn't believe it. I was asked to hold one hand out at arm's length and he struck it three times and told me to put it down. I automatically held out the other hand but he said that would suffice and he didn't want to see me in his office again. I couldn't believe I had got off so lightly and it had all happened behind closed doors with no audience. I think perhaps he took pity on me because my hand didn't hurt much either! I had never known a headmaster be so lenient. In fact the headmaster at this school was the best I'd ever known and the bullying by the other children seemed to get less as did my father's beatings at home (generally). I think he was resigning himself to the fact that I would be a dustman and had given up all hope for me.

However, immediately after this truancy episode my father got to hear of it and the next day after tea I was told to go in the spare bedroom and strip. I heard my mother telling him not to be so harsh on me, but he was soon tying my elbows together in front of me. He put a towel down in front of the large wardrobe and told me to lie on it. He then splayed my legs as far apart as they would go and tied my ankles to the bottom hinges of the double wardrobe. I then had to sit upright while he strapped my nicely rounded back until my stomach muscles weakened and my back hit the floor. I remember `coming' at that point, completely exhausted and I didn't know which hurt worse, my back or ejaculating. I knew then why he had put the towel down, because I was left tied in that position all night on the floor and I had no option but to wee all over myself and onto the towel. Luckily it was a warm night and when he untied me in the morning he said he hoped he wouldn't have to punish me again for truancy. It took me half an hour to get moving and my mother put cream on my back. I thought that was kind but where had she been when I really needed her the night before when she knew full well what my father was doing to me?

When I was 14 I was chased and caught by an all-girl gang. I was stripped and ordered to make a bridge with my body, my arms straight out on the floor and my knees at 90 degrees. I knew I couldn't hold this position for long and as I sagged a lighted cigarette was held on the ground under my bottom. I was burnt many times before my stomach muscles, legs and arms gave out and I collapsed on the ground. I was screaming and was unaware that the cigarette had been removed from under me because the pain continued. While this was happening I had `come' all over my stomach and a girl rubbed my hand in it and forced my hand all over my face, covering me with sticky semen. But I hadn't any strength to struggle and lay there feeling dirty, defenceless and humiliated. My penis hurt me so much when I ejaculated, but while it was still big, a girl tied a rope around it and I was hauled to my feet.

They then all took off their school ties and stood in a circle around me while another girl tied my wrists in front of me. I was dragged around the circle by my penis, while they whipped me with their ties all down my back and right down to my calves. Finally my penis got smaller and the rope pulled off and a girl held me with her forearm around my neck, while my wrists were released. I was punched in the stomach a few times while still in the armlock and then I sunk to the ground. They walked off saying what a cissy I was. I managed to get my clothes on before it started to rain but by the time I had walked home, I was soaked and must have looked a real mess. My father exploded at the sight of me, but fortunately he was late for a meeting and didn't have time to bother about me. I didn't say anything to my mother and slipped upstairs for a quick clean up before tea.

My mother asked me what had happened when I got down for tea, but I just said I fell over in the wet and that was it. She didn't ask any more questions and never really listened anyway. I looked at my pathetic figure in the mirror at bedtime and my back wasn't as bad as I thought it might be and it didn't look cut at all. It was my bottom that hurt most with so many cigarette burns all over it. My penis was very bruised and blackened again and hurt a lot, but as I could wee this time, I thought I would get by OK.

My father took me again to Belfast with him and put me through more of his tortures which were supposed to bring me into manhood. Once again I despaired at his total lack of compassion. How could this man, who was supposed to look after me, treat me like this, especially knowing what others did to me as well? My body rarely had time to heal from one torture before the next horror began. Looking back, it was no surprise how weak I was, but at the time I was surrounded by people constantly telling me how feeble and spineless I was so I believed them. I had no control over my penis and the pain was getting worse when I was made to ejaculate. Though my father never touched me to make this happen, he often put me in certain positions which made it inevitable. He used to do this on purpose, watch me suffer and then tell me how disgusted he was with my behaviour. My testicles rarely hung down now and were two solid lumps either side of my penis. Was I different to other boys? Was that why I was picked on? I was very confused. When my father brought me home from Belfast this time I was very disillusioned with my life and wished it would all end. Was I really that bad, or was everyone else wrong? I longed to see Gran Cook at Cheltenham for Christmas.

The school year continued with another lecture from my father saying that he wanted to see a much better report this term and more piano practice. My mother was rarely in when I returned from school as she was always out enjoying one of her many sports or hobbies. The house was so cold in winter because the fire was never lit until tea time when she got home. I had the usual bad chilblains and it took me ages to get to sleep every night. However the term finished without too much more trouble and soon we were on the road to visit Gran Cook at Cheltenham for Christmas.

My parents used to take all the food with us as Gran didn't have enough money to feed us all. They would buy some coal for her if it was running low. My mother's brothers and their families lived locally and would call round while we were there. The aunts and uncles would drink a lot and gamble on card games like Newmarket or Bridge until the early hours, although I always had to go to bed by 9.30. I remember one time when the loud voices turned to shouting and they all sounded very angry. It ended with my uncle taking an axe to Gran's Christmas tree and then throwing it outside before they all stormed out.

All my cousins were in long trousers, even the younger ones and as usual I was the odd one out in my shorts. I remember asking my father once again if I could have some long trousers as I was so cold, but he said not until I was 15 years old. I wouldn't have minded so much if I had a good figure, but I was so skinny and my legs were so thin. I was also really embarrassed at being so exposed. I always felt so cold in the winter and longed for the summer to come.

We had a great time with Gran Cook and Smutter and I was very sad when we had to come home. At least the journey was a bit quicker in the Standard Eight, but there was still no heater so the drive over the Cotswolds in winter was very cold. We needed all our warmest clothes on. I remember it was so cold when we got home that I put a thermometer in my bedroom and it registered just 25 degrees Fahrenheit, -4 centigrade! All the pipes were frozen solid so my father and I had to spend ages in the loft with warm rags trying to thaw them out.

I was so cold that I made the mistake of going to bed with my clothes on and when my father came in in the morning he was furious. He pulled all the clothes off me and asked me whatever I thought I was doing? I said I was so cold and my chilblains were itching, so I kept my socks on. He said I was a dirty, spineless, good for nothing baby and told me to strip. He took all my clothes and was soon back with the dreaded neckties and bits of rope. Each wrist was then tied to the top corners of the bed head with neckties and I was spread-eagled on my back. The ropes were then tied to my ankles and he stretched me to the limit, pulling the ropes tight around the bottom legs of the bed. My father said I would now begin to find out what being cold really felt like. He left me and I heard a big argument going on downstairs, so I thought my mother may be having a few words for me. All went quiet and I was in a lot of pain and freezing cold.

Later on another argument was heard and soon after my mother came in with more clothes and released me and said I could come down to dinner. I had been there for 4 hours. I couldn't move and my mother rubbed me to get me moving. I was dying for a wee but couldn't go. We had dinner in stony silence and my father didn't speak to me for 4 days. I finally managed to have a wee in the evening and it really burned me and hurt so much when it came out. I was glad to get to bed again that night, cold though it was, as nobody was talking to each other so at least I thought I would get some peace.

I had been in bed about half an hour when my father came in and pulled all my bedclothes off again, to make sure I wasn't wearing anything. He was standing over me with his belt in his hand and I was cowering and shaking with fear, rolled up on my side. He said he wished I could see what a pathetic, weak boy I looked and lashed me twice on my bare bottom and left. I pulled my bedclothes up over my body and felt so utterly alone.

I often thought about running away from home, as I had done from school, but I hadn't got the guts or confidence in myself at this time. Where would I run to anyway? All my spirit had been crushed long ago by the constant abuse at home and at school. I couldn't understand why I was on this earth at all? What was the point of my life? I only had my grandmothers to speak to and one of them was a long way away in Cheltenham. I began to despair more and more and longed for the time when my school days would end and I could start a new life at work. My 15th birthday was in July and I was looking forward to getting my first pair of long trousers as promised.

My father wanted me to stay on at school for another year, but I didn't want to and told him so and he was livid. It was warm in the house as the coal fire was burning for the last time before the summer. He got an upright kitchen chair and brought it in front of the fire. I had to strip and sit on the seat while he tied an ankle to each chair leg. My elbows were pulled together behind the chair back causing great pressure and pain in my shoulders and my biceps were crushed against the chair sides. He pushed me close to the fire and the sweat soon started running off me. He said that when I apologised and agreed to go back to school for another year, he would release me. I was determined not to and he pushed the chair closer to the fire and my penis got hot and bigger and I cried out in pain as I ejaculated once again with my father watching. He said that if I had been sensible I wouldn't have had to go through this performance and then my mother came in. After a blazing row she untied me. But my father still insisted that I should fill the tin bath with cold water and watched me wash myself. It was freezing after the heat of the fire. It was awful. Was there no end to the ways this man could think of to hurt and humiliate me? We ate tea in stony silence and I was kept naked and told to go to bed straight afterwards. I felt so weak and feeble and wondered whether this treatment was usual for every boy growing up? As it turned out, after all this, I had to stay on at school for another year anyway as I wasn't quite old enough to start on the apprenticeship that my father wanted me to do.

I was glad to be starting my last term at this school (I was to change school the next year) and couldn't wait for it to be over. Now that my shoulders and arms were getting stronger I was expected to do more games and PT, but I managed to convince teachers that I was still in too much pain and didn't get the cane at all for underperforming! Another blessing was that the ex-paratrooper teacher was finally sacked after a load of complaints. I remember he once pinned me to the floor in front of the class with his foot on my throat. I couldn't breathe and other girls and boys surprisingly rushed forward and pulled him off after a struggle. Luckily we had the southern area heavyweight boxing champion for his age in our class and he knocked him out! It was a great fracas and it felt incredible to have some of the kids finally sticking up for me. Many complaints had been made against him in the past which had been ignored. But now they had to expel either the whole class or him. So power came to the pupils for once! I got on much better with the replacement teacher, which was great.

I had a good day on my 15th birthday when I was finally presented with my first pair of long trousers and I was so happy with them, I couldn't believe it! I felt so much warmer and spent a lot of the day in front of the mirror trying different shirts on with them and I felt so secure. But the bad news was that my father said they were only to be worn for special occasions in the summer as they would be too warm for me until winter.

Just before the school summer term ended, my father took me to Belfast again and I remember it was a very rough crossing and the docks were crawling with armed police and troops which frightened me. It had turned cold again and I can't remember what I'd done wrong, if anything, but my father subjected me to the chair treatment again. The weather was unseasonably cold and instead of being hot in front of the fire, he watched me get colder and colder, as of course I had been stripped naked again. I was hurting badly but he just sat on the bed calmly doing some paperwork for a meeting he had next day and watched me, bound and in incredible pain for three hours. He then ran a hot bath and forced me into it which was very painful on my freezing cold body, then he hauled me out to drip dry before sending me to bed.

The end of the school year finally came and I finished 49th out of 55 in the class which I thought was good because I had never been out of the bottom 4 in my life! However my parents weren't impressed, though they did cheer up a bit when I passed another piano exam. My mother bought me the latest Dinky toy tipper truck to add to my collection and I was so pleased with it that it never left my sight. Toys from my parents were rare, even for Christmas and birthdays. I took it on holiday with me that year when we reverted back to Paignton. I was very grateful to have something to play with as sadly John and his family didn't go there anymore. I still did the exercises John had shown me and did a lot of swimming in the sea. I could still feel his encouragement from all the years before. By the time I got home I could pull myself up with my biceps while hanging from a bar and touch my chin on it. Pretty pathetic by most standards, but a physical breakthrough for me. After a long, painful struggle I had reached one of my goals in life!

One time during the holidays I was pedalling across the army ranges to see Gran Cally in Aldershot when I was knocked off my bike by a gang. There were boys and girls in the gang, some from my school and some I didn't know. I was stripped and held in a Boston crab position, while they tried to get me to say yes to joining their gang. I really didn't want to be part of their gang so I held out as long as I could and was then backed up against a tree trunk and forced to my knees with my legs pulled back and my ankles tied behind the tree. My wrists were also tied behind the tree and I was burnt with cigarettes on my testicles, chest, nipples and armpits whilst they asked me to say 'yes'. The girls roughly made me ejaculate while the boys punched me in the stomach and biceps. But I didn't say yes to joining their gang so I was quite pleased with myself. After a while they untied me and left but I was so cold and in so much pain that I could hardly dress. I managed to cycle on to Gran at the pub and as she was busy serving, I didn't have any explaining to do. I slipped down the cellar to drown my sorrows in cider. I was also developing quite a taste for ale at this age and found that either cider or ale helped to make my troubles begin to fade.

A few days later I was back with Gran Cook in Cheltenham for a few days and as usual I felt so safe and didn't want to go back to school for another dreaded year at Farnborough. However I felt more able to face it after finding some peace with Gran and Smutter again. Gran always tried to instil confidence in me and spoke with me a lot and always had time to listen to me, which my parents never did. Back at home I was just there to be seen and not heard, to be tormented at will depending on my father's mood at the time. But at least I did have Gran Cally nearby.

CHAPTER 10
Leaving School at Last

I started my final school year soon after we got back from Gran Cally's. This time I was at the large new comprehensive school in Hawley which had been formed from all the 11 to 16 year olds from the surrounding schools. This covered quite a wide area which meant that many children now had to travel on buses whereas before they could walk or cycle to their local schools. Those schools then became just primary and infant schools from reception up to 11 year olds, whereas before they were reception right through to leaving at 15 or 16. I wondered what would happen to the gang culture in a huge new school where everyone had been mixed up together from different schools and felt unnerved about it all.

We were expected to wear a uniform but as usual my father wouldn't buy one for me. But I wasn't the only one to be without as many of the army and gypsy children didn't wear one either. There was fairly intense rivalry between the pupils from different schools especially on the sports field. So the rival gangs still operated and the teachers had no idea how to handle it. But this may explain why I had been press ganged so hard during the holidays to join a gang before we started there.

But thankfully I was finally allowed to wear my long trousers so I felt much less self-conscious and wasn't nearly as exposed and vulnerable as I had been in shorts. By now I was six foot tall and as many of the children didn't know me, they didn't seem to pick on me so readily either. Some of the worst tormentors had left school at the end of the previous year, including the horrible girl who I had to sit next to. I now sat next to a boy who wasn't a member of the gangs, so I felt a bit safer. The bullying at school gradually got less in that final year, although some of the girls still enjoyed hurting me for some reason whenever they had a good chance. Another great thing about this new school was that I didn't get caned any more. I am not sure if it was used on anyone else but finally, at school at least, it had come to an end.

For some reason the girl gangs were always much more calculating and cruel in their punishments than the boy gangs. I was very afraid of any females other than my grandmothers by this time. I also noticed that by now as soon as my shoulder blades were forced to touch the ground or a wall or a tree or anything, I just went to pieces and usually couldn't help ejaculating in a very short time. This was becoming a big problem for me because it meant that I couldn't lie on my back and sunbathe in my trunks without my penis getting big. It was no better lying on my front. If my father saw me like that while we were ever on holiday he would march me into the sea up to my chest until I was frozen. He would then get me to sit on the beach in my wet costume with nothing else on for ages and laugh while he said that I couldn't function now!

Soon I wasn't able to stretch out on my back at all without problems and this was tearing me apart and making me an emotional wreck. Was I normal? I had no sex education at school or at home, it was all a dirty subject. So I had no idea what was going on with my body and why it behaved like it did. I just knew that it was a fascination to others for some reason and a horribly painful problem to me. I didn't know anything anymore and became even more fearful and withdrawn.

Thankfully though, my father was abroad for a couple of months when I started at the new school and I felt the pressure was off me for a while and I seemed to be learning a bit better as a result. I was more able to concentrate and I enjoyed my best term ever. By Christmas I was 36th out of 55, by far my best result. I was able to do my homework and exercises before my mother got in most nights, but I still struggled when I pulled myself up to touch my chin on the tree branch. No real surprise as the muscles necessary had been ripped apart long before and had never repaired properly. But I didn't realise that then, I just thought I was weak like everyone said I was.

Now that the bullying was getting less my shoulders were gradually improving and by the end of the term I could do a few press-ups and a couple of pull-ups with my chin touching the bar. Still nothing to what the other boys could do, but quite an achievement for me. My parents made me do house work and get the coal in and saw wood for the fire. This took a long time as my shoulders and arms were still not very strong and what with the gardening and the music practice, I didn't have much time to myself. Also my homework increased and when he got back, my father would give me even more. When he lost his patience with me for not getting the answers right, especially in maths and English, he would still sometimes torture and humiliate me even though I was now six foot tall and 15 years old. I was too scared to stand up to him as he was such a big strong man and at only eight stone I thought I wouldn't stand a chance anyway. My life would not have been worth living at all if I had tried to stand up to him and failed.

His favourite treatment at this time was to tell me to put my birthday suit on and sit me on a wooden chair with no back. He then tied my left ankle to my left wrist and to the left front chair leg and vice versa. This meant that I was bent over with my chest touching my knees, presenting a vulnerable rounded back. Depending on how he was feeling this could be done outside in the cold or inside in front of the hot range. Then my back would be lashed and I would be left in that position for about 2 hours The worst time I remember was in the cold in the garden when I must have passed out, after counting about 15 lashes. I was quickly brought round by being drenched with a bucket of freezing cold water and left there until I dried in the icy wind. I was so cold that when my father released me I couldn't move and thought my back would never straighten again. It was the next day before I could wee. It really burned me and hurt a lot but there was no point in telling anyone.

I survived as usual and these outbursts thankfully became fewer and soon very rare. It may have been because I finished somewhere in the twenties in my class at the end of spring term at school, which was my highest position in the class ever. My father still worked at the RAE and although I didn't want to, he said I must try for an apprenticeship there. The trouble was that apart from a few shops in Cove and North Camp, I didn't know where else to work nearby. So as I didn't know what else to do, I duly filled in the application forms and assumed that I wouldn't be invited to sit the entrance exam. I hoped that would be the end of it because even if I did do the exam, I wouldn't pass it and would definitely not pass an interview for what was considered then, one of the most sought after apprenticeships in the world!

However, to my surprise I was invited to sit the entrance exam. Although I didn't particularly want to sit the exam I was still scared when I was shown into the huge great hall with hundreds of others my age and older clutching our pencils, ruler and rubbers. I didn't bother about how I did because I didn't want it anyway and I couldn't believe it later when a very official letter was handed to me by my father, confirming that I had passed the exam and gave me a date to report for the interview. My parents were over the moon and I realised that it was the first time that I had ever seen them being really happy with me. But I didn't share their enthusiasm. I still didn't think I had a chance and now I had to go to my first interview in front of a very distinguished board of three, in a months time!

The backlash came from the other children who were much brighter than me who had failed the entrance exam. They were very hostile to me and their parents were hostile both to me and my parents. They thought I had been helped by the influence of my father working there and the position he held as head of a department. This may, or may not have been true, but again I had to suffer for it. I was caught and stripped and tied to trees and railings on many occasions, while the gangs beat and abused me, wanting me to confess that it was rigged. I was quite pleased with myself for enduring the pain and humiliation without giving in to them for a change.

I'll never forget going to the interview. The board of three, with the chairman in the middle, asked me all sorts of questions from my hobbies to maths and wanting my views on different happenings in world events and politics. The other hopefuls were huddled outside discussing it afterwards and they didn't seem very confident at all. I left quickly and tried to forget about it.

The final outcome, was that I received another official letter saying that I had been offered a five year Craft Apprenticeship with time part time studying at the RAE Technical College, to take the City and Guilds courses to qualify as an engineer. It also stated that this depended on obtaining a good final report from school, so I'm afraid the pressure was still on me to obtain a good class position in my final term. I couldn't believe I had managed it and wondered if my father's position at RAE had influenced my chances after all. Only one other boy had got in from my school despite many applying. I felt quite pleased with myself for a change for achieving something better than the rest of them. My teachers had always said that I would be a dustman, just as my father had repeatedly told me.

I was only stripped and tied to the chair with no back and beaten by my father once more in all my last term at school and that was for not practicing the piano enough. I had a Grade 7 Higher piano examination coming up in my school holidays. That must have been a record and without this abuse at his hands, my body was finally and gradually able to become stronger. When the term ended my report was the best ever and I had risen to the dizzy heights of second in my class out of 51! Maybe the teacher was on my side after all? I wonder what heights I could have achieved if I had not had any of the abuse to scramble my young brain and had had less time off school for injuries and illness?

Everyone was so pleased except me. This was considered passable enough by the RAE to accept me to start the apprenticeship in September, but I still didn't want to go. I also managed to pass the piano exam just before I went to Paignton again for our holiday. It was a good holiday and everyone was much more relaxed than before and I could feel my shoulders and body strengthening with the swimming once more and I came back very refreshed.

It was after this last trip to Paignton, and before I started work, that I was caught by the dreaded mixed gang for the last time, while I was struggling to do my pull ups on a tree branch in the woods. It was a lovely hot August day and I was only wearing my shorts, socks and shoes, as I had taken my T- shirt off to do my pull up exercises. They quickly stripped me and forced me to the ground on my back. They held my arms and legs tightly and pinched my nose to make my mouth open. Then they each weed in my face, making me struggle to breathe and blinding me in incredible pain as it sprayed in my eyes. They then threw me over onto my front. My arms were brought up over my shoulders and my wrists tied together behind my head. Both legs were pulled up behind my back and the ankles tied together with the rope from my wrists, bending me backwards like a banana. I fell over on my side and the girls tickled me as I was writhing about and burnt my armpits and bottom with cigarettes.

My ankles were then untied and I was dragged to a tree, were I was tightly tied to the trunk by my waist, my wrists still tied behind my head. The boys then pulled my legs as far apart as possible, while the girls pulled and squeezed my penis until I ejaculated in their hands and they wiped it all over my face and hair. They spat in my face and taunted me about my puny body and said I wouldn't be released until I admitted I was a coward and spineless, and that I wouldn't say anything to anyone about this happening. My biceps and stomach were punched as the girls tried to get my penis big for a second time and I was taunted for not being able to. I hadn't even the strength to plead for mercy when the boys said I had had enough and pulled the big girl away from my penis. The boys released my wrists and waist and they all went off laughing as I slumped to the ground covered in sweat as the tree was in full sun. I finally got dressed, but I knew that my biceps were not going to be practicing any pull ups for a while. At least there was no one at home when I arrived, so I was able to clean myself up and put a long sleeved shirt on so it would hide the bruises on my biceps and stomach before my parents came in. If they had seen, I would have been in for more taunting for not sticking up for myself, so it was best just hidden away.

A lot of the last school holiday in my life was spent at Aldershot with Gran Cally in the pub and I'm afraid I was drinking beer and cider most of the time and had developed quite a taste for it! At least I felt safe there and enjoyed myself and had a good laugh when my Gran had to throw the soldiers out on a Sunday lunch time when they didn't want to go home. The holiday was nearly over when I also received the last physical punishment from my father. My parents and I were sunbathing in the garden and I had my swimming trunks on, not a pretty sight! I hadn't long been lying on my back when the pressure of the costume on my penis made it come big and it popped out the top of my costume and ejaculated over my stomach. To my horror both my parents saw it happen and I was told to go to my bedroom by my father.

I had taken my trunks off and was cleaning myself up when my father came in. He said he had never seen such a dirty, filthy exhibition of sexual behaviour in all his life and he wouldn't tolerate it from a son of his. He said I was very fortunate because he couldn't mark me, as I had a medical appointment for the apprenticeship in a couple of days. But I would still be taught a lesson I would never forget for acting in such a despicable way. He tied me in the same position as the mixed gang had done a few weeks earlier and left me helpless on my side on the hard floor. He said my wrists were on a slipknot and he would be back to tighten me up later. I could hardly breathe as it was, but he came back four times to tighten the rope between my ankles and wrists and I was bent farther back each time, with my penis being most vulnerable. I heard a lot of arguing downstairs and later my mother appeared with a knife and cut the rope, for the first time ever.

That hurt even more and my mother massaged me until she was able to get my legs and arms from behind my back. It was very painful and when she had got me lying on my back gasping for air, I ejaculated again. Thankfully she didn't say anything but cleaned me up and got me to a sitting position propped up by the side of the bed. She left me and came back with tea and cakes and I managed to feed myself but I couldn't hold the cup still as my hands were shaking so much, so she held it while I drank. She helped me into bed and I don't remember any more until morning. I was frightened to move at first, but was very relieved when I felt much better than I thought I would. Walking wasn't too bad either and by the time I went for the medical at the RAE I felt quite normal again. I wondered whether I would get through the medical and was very afraid when I was asked to take all my clothes off and was prodded all over the place.

I was stretched on my back on the couch and once again I ejaculated while a male doctor was feeling my groin area but amazingly nothing was said. I think he could see my fear. A few days later the letter came giving me the all clear for the medical and a starting date and where to report and what to take with me, such as two boiler suits. My father had a fit as he said one boiler suit cost a small fortune and I would have to make do with that and buy the other out of my wages. No helping hand from him in spite of me gaining the place he wanted me to have against the odds and against my wishes.

It was only many years later, when I was in my mid 40s, I learnt that 'coming' was a perfectly natural and normal experience and is meant to be enjoyed. But my earliest experience of it, not knowing anything, was when the girl gangs made it happen to me and it hurt a lot. My parents always treated this act as a dirty subject and wouldn't speak about it with me. In fact my father, who should have been helping me to know what was going on, would punish me for it and that added to my fear and shame. We had no sex education at school in those days so I had no idea of what was going on.

I also had no idea why my father or the gangs took such delight in making it happen to me, except that it caused me such pain and they enjoyed anything that caused me pain. I had tried talking to the doctor but he was no help and I didn't know who else to turn to for advice. So I just endured it all as another torture and suffered well into my adult life with fear of what was happening to me. Because of the treatment I had endured at the hands of so many females, girls, matrons and nurses, it put me off ever having a proper relationship with a woman. I never had any close friends to talk to about such things either. So I never learned how a boy's body changes into a mans the way that most boys eventually find out, one way or another.

I wasn't looking forward to starting work at all because I didn't know what to expect and I felt very insecure. I felt in a way that I had been trapped into a five-year apprenticeship, which seemed a very long time to me if I didn't like it. It may have been better had I had any confidence, but I was afraid of just about everyone and specially scared of girls. I wondered if there would be any bullying there, like at school. However the starting date in September 1956 arrived and I pedalled to my first day's work in the big wide world with my boiler suit, pen and pencils. I was finally free from school, but in my heart I was fearing the worst, as the worst had so often happened to me before. What would this next chapter in life hold for me? In actual fact my life did finally take a turn for the better and my apprenticeship turned out to be a real turning point for me.

Epilogue

After finishing this book and while editing it, one of my godsons suggested that I should perhaps take a moment to reflect on how I think about my childhood now, looking back at it and the people involved.

Looking back on my childhood takes me to a very dark place with my grandmothers and holidays supplying my only source of light. I often stood naked in front of my bedroom mirror wishing I had a more muscular, stronger body so that I could stand up to the bullies. I hated my body and despite exercising until I dropped, my body never improved and I became so discouraged. As an adult looking back I can now understand that the many injuries inflicted on me as a growing child all left their marks on my body. As my body never had the chance to heal properly from one torture session to the next it is no surprise that I was always so weak. But I didn't see that then and nor did they. I just thought, why me? Why am I so weak and continually being punished at home and school? Am I really as bad as my parents and teachers make out? What have I really done to deserve all this punishment? Am I as thick as they all tell me I am? My trouble was that because this rhetoric was all I heard, I began to believe it. After all, as a child I believed what my parents and teachers said, so my self-esteem was nil. I felt I was worthless and had no value. It seemed the whole world was against me and no one wanted to listen to me because it wasn't what they wanted to hear. I was written off as being no good and the only people who cared about me and listened to me were my grandmothers.

I felt like I was different from everyone else in some way because people, especially other children, seemed to be able to pick up on my vulnerability. They knew I was an easy target, and I felt that I had the word "VICTIM" tattooed on my forehead for everyone to see. I have spoken about my past with other survivors of abuse who felt that they too were labelled "VICTIM" and everyone else could somehow see it. An awful thing I found from talking to other abuse survivors was how the abuse from their parents often continued into their adult years; it just changed form. The physical abuse they remember as children was exchanged for mental abuse by their parents, or partners when they reach adulthood. Even when they had married and raised a family, their parents still victimised them and treated them like dirt. Still nothing they said or did was right. One lovely lady I know who nears retirement now and has raised a wonderful family, has admitted to me that the best day of her life will be when her mother dies. I can so relate to her feelings, as I felt that the best day of my life was when my father died. The only difference between her and myself is that she is still suffering at her age, but I was able to start a new life aged 44.

The above example is from my experience of sharing with others and is not unfortunately an isolated case. We must all be aware that there are predators amongst us who are able to pick up on some people's vulnerability and use it for their own evil desires. I have no idea how they know who is vulnerable and who is not, but some people pick up on it far too easily.

As I have mentioned before, I have never been good at trusting people, and I put a lot of that down to the abuse inflicted on me. I'm still wary of females, so I have never got close enough to any one of them to fall in love. Because of this I used to think that there was something wrong with me and I'm sure many others did too. However I now know that becoming insular was my way of protecting myself from ever being a victim again. I've often thought that I may have missed out on some good times being married, but speaking with others has convinced me that I have escaped some bad times too.

A question that stood out for me whilst writing this book was "Why were so many people carrying ropes about with them?" My thoughts take me back to the children's Saturday morning pictures I used to attend in the cinema at that time. The vast majority of the films shown were different takes on Cowboys and Indians or United States Troopers and Indians fighting each other. I saw a lot of torture positions in these films that I was subjected to. This leads me to believe that the children picked up on this and tried it out on other children like me. Maybe that should show us the impact of what young children fill their minds with.

What they didn't understand was the extent of the pain they were inflicting on me. I think the boys understood this more than the girls as they seemed to want to release me sooner than the girls ever did. Of course in these films the tortured victims, more often than not, were able to walk away after being freed. But that is not what happens in real life. Quite the opposite in fact as people can be scarred for life. My chest is permanently sunken in due to the muscles being torn apart when they hung me in the tree. The emotional damage left equally deep scars. Although with love, care, a lot of encouragement from real friends, support from my new family and professional counselling, I have been able to overcome much of the emotional damage.

Sadly this abuse still goes on today under a different guise. The only difference being that the ropes have been replaced by knives and guns. The films may explain the children's interest in ropes, but why my father used them on me so much I will never know. I suspect he must have just got a kick out of seeing me suffer for some reason. He even made a special wooden "A" frame to tie me up to in various different positions to increase the pain. I could maybe have understood him lashing out at me in temper or frustration, but he obviously put a lot of thought into what he was going to do to me the next time. Also, I have never understood why my mother didn't intervene to help me more than she did as she knew a lot of what he did to me. Perhaps she was scared of him too. I will never know.

Having had my spirit completely crushed in my childhood I became somewhat of a loner at school and the RAE apprenticeship thankfully presented a completely different world for me. I went from being seen and not heard at school and home, to now having teachers who wanted to hear what I had to say. Although I originally didn't want to do the apprenticeship, it was the making of me. With my release from continual fear I gradually grew in confidence and the five years which I first thought was a life sentence, was actually the beginning of a much better life for me.

To this day I am still very wary of females and can count my real friends of that gender on one hand. I was in my middle forties when a loving family took me under their wing just after they had got married. They later then asked me if I would like to be their sons' godfather. For the first time since my grandmothers died I at last felt that I could trust someone and that they trusted me. Several people tried to persuade them that I should not be left alone with their sons believing that as I had been abused as a child I was more than likely to abuse other children. I was so angry at this. I knew the pain of being abused so I was the last person to want to inflict it on anyone else, least of all my precious godsons. Thankfully their parents trusted me and I was so pleased to accept their offer.

Having had no experience of little children, I was quite apprehensive of how I would fare as a godfather and I didn't want to let my new family down. All I did know for sure was that I would do my utmost to make sure that the boys' childhoods would be much happier than mine. Happily my fears vanished as soon as the eldest was born and I gelled with both of them right from the start.
Knowing these boys right from their birth, seeing how they were brought up and being part of it completely changed my life. It gave me something special to live for instead of just my work. It also showed me that the making of fine young men is brought about through love, encouragement, support and lots of fun times. Not with the torment and lies that my own father told me would make me into a man.

Now I think of myself as a survivor of abuse rather than a victim of it. I could not have overcome my traumas without the help of a loving family and a few very dedicated friends. I thank God daily for leading me to each one of them. They were the ones who had faith in who I could be and not who I had been made to be. Some of my healing came about through many hours of specific prayer over certain memories that still haunted me and robbed me of sleep well into my adulthood.

I think all victims, mostly, need someone to spend time with them, to value them, draw close to them and just listen. My new family, friends and the counsellor did that for me and talked me through from being a victim to being a victor. My godsons brought me a new life, a new beginning, and helped me to find the peace of mind and enjoyment of life that I have today.

I pray that this book will give hope and encouragement to any readers who have been through abuse themselves. I also hope that it shows everyone who reads it, the value of caring for and listening to those we meet. Some people have not known much kindness and have never been able to trust people because of bad experiences in their past. But if we all offer the hand of friendship to those around us, in doing so we can change their lives forever and give them hope.

Edward Bruce

Printed in Great Britain
by Amazon